I WASN'T BORN TO GO HOME, AND NEITHER WERE YOU

FINDING YOUR GIFT, FACING LIFE'S CHALLENGES, AND NEVER TAKING THE CHICKEN EXIT

NABIL CHERIF

EMILY CHERIF

STREAMLINE
BOOKS

I WASN'T BORN TO GO HOME, AND NEITHER WERE YOU

Finding Your Gift, Facing Life's Challenges, and Never Taking the Chicken Exit

Cover Design by Will Severns

Streamline Books

www.WriteMyBooks.com

Paperback ISBN: 9-798-3702-0534-7

Hardcover ISBN: 9-798-3751-2541-1

January 21st, 2023

To Emily, my wife, without her I would not be who I am today.

To Fatima, my mother (Ommi), first business partner and believer in me from the day I was born. I'm doing my best to live up to the meaning of my name: noble, do the right thing.

To You, dear reader, to let you know that our stories matter. To remind you that your name is a unique gift to you. I encourage you, as Ommi did for me, "Go, live up to the meaning of your name."

ABOUT THE TITLE

The chicken exit greets you right before you enter the roller coaster car queue. Before you sit down and pull the lap bar tight against your waist, it is the sign that points in the opposite direction. Your nerves and jitters too much to overcome, this exit offers you the last chance to bail out and head home. How many times have you faced this exit? Did you take it, or did you press on?

This is the journey of a man who ignored the exit sign each time it was presented. It is a story of times when he was admonished, and cautioned repeatedly, to turn around and go home. Like the time, while en route, Nabil was advised to skip his final meeting of the day by being told, "you can just go home now, the proposal was not granted." He immediately responded, "I wasn't born to go home" and drove to the building anyway, and secured five more contract opportunities! All because Nabil didn't take the chicken exit—this book will explain why you should do the same.

Contents

Contents

FOREWORD I

BY BRIAN MINER

One Sunday morning in 2000 a family in our church brought a visitor with them. The visitor was a young man from Tunisia who was introduced to me as Nabil. Life is a journey filled with unexpected twists and turns. We did not realize it at the time, but Nabil and I had both just made a major change in the path that our lives would follow from this meeting forward. Over the twenty-two years that have passed since that first meeting, we have traveled a path of personal and cultural change that neither of us could have possibly foreseen at the time.

Nabil had come to the States to pursue additional education. I had come to church confident and comfortable in the belief that my life would continue much as it had always been working in my small business and serving as a Deacon in the same church that my wife and I had attended for almost our entire married life. The possibility that I might end up working and ministering cross culturally was just as far from my imagination as entrepreneurship and U.S. citizenship were from Nabil's. And yet this is exactly where our journey has taken us.

The path has not been an easy one. Nabil was very naive about life in the States. Like many who come to the States, he would discover that this country is no utopia and, just like any other place, it is only through hard work and sacrifice that anyone can hope to accomplish their dreams. Meanwhile, I was very comfortable in my Midwestern cocoon of comfort and security. Starting in 2004 I would travel to Haiti many times, learn a new language, move my family to a Haitian American church in our hometown and start learning just how different life is for most of the people in the world. In the process my wife and I have learned and grown in ways that we never could have on our own. As Nabil struggled to make the transition from being a young Tunisian salesman to being an entrepreneurial American, I was there with him along the way. As I struggled to make the transition from being an insular Midwesterner to doing cross cultural ministry in a developing country, Nabil was there with me all along the way. Nabil speaks English fluently after all these years in the States but he also speaks French as a second language while I speak Haitian Creole as a second language. We often carry-on conversations in French and Haitian Creole despite the fact that we are both fluent in English. I can understand about 75% of what Nabil says to me in French and he can understand about 75% of what I say to him in Creole but neither one of us can speak the other's language and fully understand what the other is saying. These conversations are something of a microcosm of our entire relationship.

We are constantly seeking to communicate and understand each other as good friends always do, but we are never quite able to fully overcome the gulf created by our very different backgrounds. The key to getting as far as we have in our journey together is that we have persevered and we have always regarded the differences that make it so hard to truly understand each other as being some of the most valuable things that each of us brings to our friendship.

Readers of this book might be a little intimidated about embarking on a journey that leads to unforeseen and sometimes daunting places. After all, our journey is taking us to rural Haiti to do development work. I could have just politely introduced myself to Nabil on that Sunday morning in 2000 and Nabil would have been fully justified had he written me off as too deeply rooted in my ways to be worth pursuing as a friend. But our journey through life as friends has been a profound blessing and help to both of us and neither of us would trade it for any other path. This is why I encourage you to read Nabil's story and seek to better understand the possibilities that exist for following a very different path through this life. Then, once you have read this book, open up your heart and your mind to the people that come into your life. Be willing to listen and to share honestly and openly. Embrace new ideas and possibilities. I cannot promise that it will be easy, but I can promise that such a path will be very rewarding. Just remember, when you find a friend, no matter how rough the going gets, hold onto your friendship as you make your journey through this life.

—Brian Miner

FOREWORD II

BY DON AND JEAN HESS

I count it a privilege to share about my relationship with a man who, I truly believe, personifies the realization of the "American Dream." Nabil was born and raised in Tunisia and emigrated to America in 2000 with little else than his faith – and the belief that this was the land where God's plan for his life could be more fully realized. My wife, Jean, and I first met Nabil at a social gathering where we learned of his story. Later, in response to our invitation, and in the dead of winter, Nabil parked his 1994 RV (his place of residence at the time) on our land referred to as "Hobbit Hollow," a beautiful little valley south of Kansas City. Due to some truly frigid weather, we invited Nabil to come in out of the cold! In the coming weeks, we had the privilege of getting much better acquainted.

At that time Nabil was beginning to put into practical use his unique mastery of several languages (Arabic, French, plus several Arabic dialects). There is an ongoing – and often urgent – need for language interpretation and translation by hospitals, social services, courts and other public services and private businesses. Nabil proved to be the man for the job, and in 2007 launched Bridging the Gap Interpreting, LLC. This service, under Nabil's highly capable leadership, began growing and today has expanded to over 100 languages and over 500 linguists all across the country.

Nabil's influence and impact took a monumental leap in 2013 when he met a lovely young lady, Emily, from Costa Rica. Their friendship soon turned to true love, and they were married in the spring of 2014. If, perchance, there are any poetry lovers reading this, we've included the following:

Nabil & Emily
Once there was just the two of you,
But now you two have become one.
Now it's a whole new kind of race,
That the Lord has called you to run.
Nabil, God calls you to love Emily
In the same way that He loves you;
He laid down His life for you and me,
And now that's what you must do, too!
Some husbands let it go to their heads,
That God appointed them to be leader!
But it means you must put her needs first,
And to cherish her, and spiritually feed her.
Emily, your role is to love, and to comfort,
And to submit to this, well, imperfect man!
You're to be there for him when he's down,
And To cheer him on and to be his best fan!
So rejoice, you two, in your new life together,

And do all you do for God's honor and glory,
Then you will surely be fulfilling your roll,
In His kingdom and in His wondrous story!

Nabil and Emily's union has provided living proof of King Solomon's ancient maxim (according to a modern translation): "Two people are better off than one, for they can help each other succeed." Emily's expertise in the area of interior decorating has turned their home and office into a warm and welcoming environment that people love to come to. Both Emily and Nabil also share the gift of hospitality and have consistently reached out in love to neighbors and countless others over the years.

Together, Nabil and Emily are living proof of the validity of Isadore Share's observation: "The reason for our success is no secret. It comes down to one single principle that transcends time and geography, religion and culture. It's the Golden Rule – the simple idea that if you treat people well, the way you would like to be treated, they will do the same."

Blessings to both of you!

—Don and Jean Hess

FOREWORD III

BY RICHARD D MOREHOUSE

"When pigs fly!" is an expression invoked when conjuring an incredulous outcome. However, over the years that I have known Nabil, I have come to understand the phrase as a brilliant example of how the simple act of trying can impact lives for the better. As a business integrator with 20 years of experience, I can say with confidence that there is something rare about Nabil's approach to life, and to business. Like most entrepreneurs, he is an amalgam of action and expressive ideation, but he also includes a steadfast belief that 95% of the goals we did not reach could have been achieved, if we had passed by the chicken exit. As you journey through the pages of *I Wasn't Born to Go Home*, you will read tangible examples of how Nabil's resolve to ignore the chicken exit sign has resulted in squadrons of flying pigs! Through these pages, you will come to realize that the biggest example of Nabil's difference is his belief in you, dear reader. He has faith that you were not born to go home, without ever trying. Furthermore, he believes in you, even when you may not believe in yourself.

Nabil believes that if you want to go fast, go alone, but as a team, you can go far. I learned this lesson as an Airman in the United States Air Force (*home to the sometimes cantankerous "flying pig", the A10 Warthog*). I was assigned to the Fightin' Fifty Fifth, Combat Applications Squadron, Strategic Air Command. As a member of the 55th Rapid Exploitation and Dissemination Team, tasked with the verification of the world's nuclear intercontinental ballistic missile inventory, and later assigned to the 55th Tactical Air Command, responsible for targeting and destroying surface-to-air missile sites during Operation Desert Storm, teamwork was critical. When I began my career in business, I learned that teamwork extended too to the Fortune 500 companies, and small and medium-sized companies for which I worked. There was something missing, however, and as I functioned in roles ranging from a member of a small team to roles where I was solely responsible for business decisions affecting hundreds of employees, I finally landed on it when I had the opportunity to work with entrepreneurs. Irrespective of whether you are interested in owning your own business or not, *I Wasn't Born to Go Home* is a gentle nudge, away from the chicken exit, and on to the challenge.

I have been blessed with the opportunity to have received a formal education, holding undergraduate and graduate degrees (MBA '23) alike. However, to be clear, my experience and applied education working with at least 200+ entrepreneurs (*in a direct capacity, a consulting capacity, or in a partnership-venture capacity*), has resulted in my most fundamental education. The Small Business Association (shorturl.at/kyY03) reports that America's economy is made up of small businesses. 2019 data from the U.S. Census Bureau shows a total of

6.1 million employer firms, 99.7% of which are businesses with less than five hundred employees. I am well informed of this threshold, as I was previously the President of a Minnesota printing and packaging company that reached levels of five hundred employees (seasonally adjusted). However, the percentage and number of employees becomes more stunning when the data is further examined, because astoundingly, firms with fewer than 10 employees make up 78.5% of the U.S. employers! The point of analyzing this data is to highlight the significance of America's entrepreneurs. They represent the backbone of the U.S. economy. One could credibly argue that entrepreneurs also represent the legs on which the economy runs, and the arms embracing the entire system. Nabil, and his company, Bridging the Gap Interpreting LLC, is part of this architecture, and *I Wasn't Born to Go Home* is chock-full with entrepreneurial examples for you, dear reader, to experience.

Happenstance is one way to describe my introduction to Nabil. My family and I had recently moved into a neighborhood at the far western edge of Wyandotte County, in Kansas City, Kansas. The area is a bucolic balance of cows, horses, seasonal flocks of Canadian Geese, and blinking fireflies. It is also where you will find a historic golf course which once hosted a foursome match between Harold "Jug" McSpaden, and Lord Byron Nelson, versus Arnold Palmer, and Jack Nicklaus, and a NASCAR speedway that occasionally invokes a reverberating Broadway-like curtain call, as 75,000 spectators urge drivers to push their engines one more lap, before summer draws to a close. It was in this setting that Nabil walked by my home. We simply waved an acknowledgement to each other. After a few more times, we upgraded to verbal "hellos," and then one day he challenged me to start jogging with him. Shortly thereafter, early one morning, even before the rooster down the road woke up, our relationship began in earnest. We moved from jogging to running sprints, to push-ups and jump rope. Then we began to include a martial arts game that I am sure he made up. The competition involved Nabil darting around me like a hornet, slapping me on the shoulders, and knees, all while I tried in vain to catch him. It was all playful fun, of course. Unless you consider getting "stung" less than a fun time! Beyond exercising, Nabil and I spent hours talking. We talked about life, cultures, languages, families, business, collectivism, religion, leadership, food, books, podcasts, anything that came to mind in those early mornings. I learned about Nabil's aspirations, and his dreams, one of which was to become an author.

His book, he told me, would not just be a book about how his life started in a tiny North African village in Tunisia. Or how he emigrated to America. Nor would it focus solely on his explorations of the United States, some by car, most by RV, before settling right in the middle, in Kansas. It would not simply be a book of how he bootstrapped himself through college, or how he harnessed his linguistic skills, in Arabic and French, to start his own firm. This book, he said, would be written to help others, some like him not born in the United States, and others, like me for instance, who were. Everyone, he said, would find support in the story of an entrepreneurial spirit, one in which the American experiment can help foster. In essence, it was a book to help, not a self-help book per se, but a guide to help others past the blinking chicken exit sign.

As Nabil and I became better acquainted, I began to learn more about his company, Bridging the Gap Interpreting, LLC. My knowledge pertaining to language services agencies was limited. Furthermore, I did not know the difference between an interpreter and a translator, I thought they were synonymous. However, as Nabil is wont to do, he quickly introduced me to the industry. From the moment I heard Nabil say, "there is nothing better than being understood," I got it. I immediately recognized the importance of providing language services to those in need. I also grasped the difference between being heard, versus being understood, and it was this gap that his company bridged. Once you see an interpreter deployed to help someone in need, it is impossible to unsee. I did not know at the time that what I was witnessing, and have since come to appreciate, was the Heart of the Interpreter®.

Around the time that Nabil introduced me to the language industry, he also introduced me to his wife, Emily Cherif. Emily reflects the pure intent of the interpreter's heart, which is partly expressed by one's desire to help others through the gift of language. She was raised in a household where her Costa Rican born Mom spoke only Spanish. Not because she did not speak English, but because she wanted her children to have the gift of bilingualism. Emily took that gift and used it to become a certified courtroom interpreter, one of the most intellectually taxing channels for professional interpreters. Emily is an accomplished professional, and it extends to all areas including how she prepares for her court sessions. This professionalism and preparation meant that she was well known within the Missouri court system, and just as cream rises to the top, so did Emily. Her talent did not go unnoticed, and Emily was hired to become part of the interpreter training team for Bridging the Gap Interpreting LLC.

You will notice, dear reader, as you progress through the book, that Emily's words become more frequent, and evident. From the moment that Nabil met Emily, he knew she was the one. Emily, on the other hand, was more deliberate, but they both arrived at the same conclusion, they were meant for each other. Similarly, when Nabil and Emily married, she was faced with another deliberate decision, should she become involved with Bridging the Gap Interpreting LLC, or should she remain on her own journey? She chose to help, and as such, the business flourished. Emily is Nabil's confidant, collaborator, promoter, protector, and his partner in life. In the same year that Nabil was born, The Rolling Stones released a song about wants and needs, and for most of us, getting what we want is nothing in comparison to receiving what we need. For Nabil, Emily is the rare example of not only getting what he wanted, but exactly what he needed. If one is keeping track, this is yet another gap that Nabil has bridged. Nabil and Emily are excellent examples of teamwork. They lift each other up in ways that enhance not only their lives but the lives of others. This book is but one more example of how they accomplished this feat. Working together, often in the wee hours of the morning, they operated as a team. Writing is not easy, and Nabil and Emily pushed, supported, and held each other accountable to create, and in doing so they have been able to achieve the result that you, dear reader, are holding. This is yet another tangible example of Nabil, and Emily both, bridging the gap.

So here we are, but before you begin this tour through the ensuing pages in earnest, I encourage you to "let go of the vine." What does this mean? Letting go of the vine is an exercise in trust, and remember the true essence of trust is that it is granted, not earned. Trust that what you will read has mean-ing, in small ways, and in much bigger ways. Trust that the stories offered here are not meant to be a topographical map where "X marks the spot," but rather a credible example of how taking a step forward, rather than taking the chicken exit, turning around, and going home, (*and perhaps never receiving the opportunity again*) can lead to achieving the goals that until today, have been only dreams. This, dear reader, is the defini-tion of letting go of the vine, and this book can help by showing you how the core values of Fairness, Empathy, Enrich-ment, and Drive (FEED) are the ingredients that Nabil, Emily, and Bridging the Gap Interpreting, LLC uses daily. Of course, this is a challenge by choice, and ok, maybe there aren't flocks of winged porcine, but what if a healthy portion of FEED is all that is needed to give us a lift? What if what we thought was magic, were the lessons found within this book, and that they were enough to help us feel like we were flying?

—Richard D Morehouse, PHR, MBA ('23)

SECTION ONE: DRIVE (BE DETERMINED; FOR YOURSELF AND OTHERS)

BORN WITH A GIFT

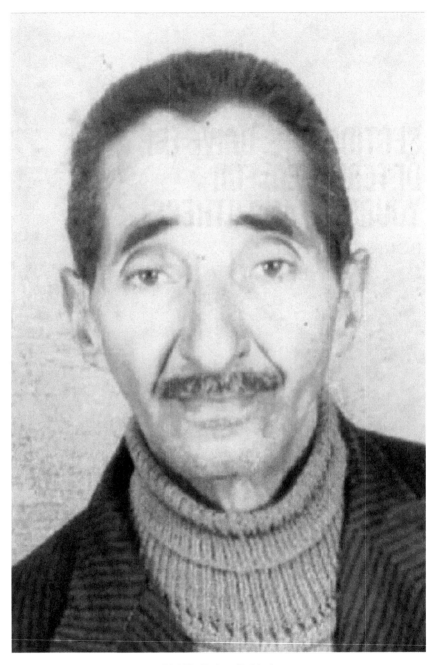

Nabil's Father (Babba)

CHAPTER 1
LE FOOTBALL

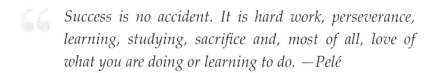
Success is no accident. It is hard work, perseverance, learning, studying, sacrifice and, most of all, love of what you are doing or learning to do. —Pelé

I was born in 1969, in the village of Col des Ruines in the mountainous city of Ain Draham in Tunisia, North Africa. Ain Draham is near the Algerian border, and its name refers to the nearby mineral rich hot springs that for centuries soothed and relaxed venturers and locals alike. Of course, as a child, I had little interest in relaxing, I was a Tunisian after-all and Tunisia is a soccer obsessed country.

As children, our objective was to move from crawling to running as quickly as possible to start playing soccer, which we did so with make-shift soccer balls, in record time!

I was the youngest of 13 children—six of which were born of my father before he was widowed, then seven more when he later married my mother. I came as a little bit of a surprise—five years after the rest! There are some downsides to being the youngest in a large family but overall the benefits were great. All of my siblings watched out for me, especially after my father passed away unexpectedly when I was only two-years-old.

In my culture, when someone passes away, they are mourned for 40 days and then left to rest without reverential mention again. Years later, as an adult, I carried the emptiness in my heart of not knowing my *Babba* (father). I was determined to face my pain and go "meet" him in my hometown. Fifty years after his passing, I was in my home-town and asked two trusted family members to take me to where he was buried because I was never told where he was laid to rest. It is a day that I will never forget because of the pain I felt then extreme relief and peace that came afterwards. I finally had the conversation I always wanted with *Babba*—are you proud of me and who I've become? I had so many other questions and no one to ask them to. To see his beautiful headstone made me feel like I truly did have a dad and for the first time, felt his covering over me and was anchored. I encourage you to go hand-in-hand with a trusted friend to face a pain you may have been avoiding too. You won't regret your decision!

Tunisia's national soccer team is known as the Eagles of Carthage. As one might expect, I was identical to many Tunisian children with progressing large motor skills, which meant running included doing so while dribbling a soccer ball. Even if we didn't have a real soccer ball, including myself, we would construct them from old clothes and rags, wrapped in plastic bags, expertly shaped and secured with ropes and Scotch Tape. My make-do ball could only heroically withstand the punishment for so long before bursting open to reveal its fabric contents. For me, it was just a matter of fact that I would need to roll and squish everything back into shape again so that the rope could be retightened and the tape reapplied. It was all great fun, but I do remember the first gift I asked for as a kid was a real soccer ball! I wanted to back myself up with options while I saved up for one myself. From the time I was six years old, I figured the best way to get what I wanted was finding ways to make a little money here and there. I would save my money in my wooden box, or under my pillow or mattress, or even in my socks. I learned the hard way, however, that socks were not the best hiding place since the bills got wet with sweat!

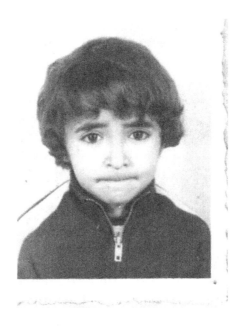

On one particularly scorching hot summer day, my brother Monji, was working in our backyard, hammering a post into the dry, red clayey soil with a sledge hammer. As he worked, his exertion became more evident with each swing, as sheets of sweat poured down his forearms. Ever the curious one, I stepped closer to him with each swing, and on the final swing the hammer slipped out of his hands and crashed onto my head. It hurt just as one might imagine a solid iron hammer landing on your head would feel, terribly. I started to cry, and

Monji, knowing that I was always saving money, and out of an abundance of caution to prove to himself that I was indeed going to be ok, quickly thought of a solution. He gave me 5 TND (Tunisian Dinars), to stop my tears. It worked! He was relieved I wasn't badly hurt and I was more than happy to add to my collection of TND.

Saving for a soccer ball was hard work, and on more than one occasion, my mission was sidetracked ever so slightly, giving way to other things that I loved, cookies! Not just any cookie would do, it needed to be Chocotom's. Founded in 1949, the TOM biscuit company is one of the oldest biscuit manufac-turers in Tunisia, and Chocotom is the flagship item for the brand. The Chocotom messaging was "it remains a myth for some, and a legend for others," but for me it was neither, I just enjoyed eating them with milk. I also enjoyed using my treasured TND for yogurt, Nestlé cheese wedges, and baguette sandwiches filled with delicious *halwa* and butter. I would also offer my Dinars to my *Ommi* (mother) if she needed something. The fact was, I loved making, saving, spending or giving away money. My family always said how good I was with money and how amazing it was that I found ways to make it since I was very young.

Earning money was fun, but I absolutely loved negotiating for it too! One time, Monji, perhaps as a result of the previous TND he had given me, which I must say was rightly earned and I had the indented scar on the top of my head to show for it, asked me for 10 TND. I had 20 TND saved, so I did give him the 10 TND, but my repayment was 25 TND once he got paid! My family was shocked over what I would say to negotiate, but to this day, all I can say is that I was born with this instinct.

From the start we can see that this, then, is the beginning story of a natural born salesman. It is one of my gifts, and I'm very proud of it! I will always love selling things and services of value, but that is only one part of what I want to share with you as it relates to the journey and successes my gift has taken me. My gift has brought me to this very precise inflection point, the point where you and I are able to connect on a singular level so that I may express this one simple truth to you: I believe you were born to succeed! With all my heart, I believe that all of us, through the special gifts we are each born with, and the unique journeys that come as a result, have the power to succeed and do so with the grace and strength to help others along our way.

My core desire is that as you read this story, you are able to see points along my pathway that resemble your own. In doing so, you will begin to understand that success is not just something bestowed to others, but it can be yours too. For instance, many of us view "success" as living out a life in the sweet spot of what we love and what we're gifted to do. Pelé defines it, as stated in our opening quote, "Success is no accident. It is hard work, perseverance, learning, studying, sacrifice and most of all, love of what you are doing or learning to do."

Pelé was our hero as kids! Whenever any of us had the soccer ball at our feet—in a field or schoolyard—we'd yell out "Pelé, Pelé, Pelé!" to whoever had the ball at the time. Pelé's given name was Edson. His birth coincided with the electrification of his hometown of Três Corações, Brazil. So, although the spelling is different, his parents named him after the famous American inventor Thomas Edison. On the other hand, Pelé is a nickname given to him by his classmates, and he hated it! However, the more vocal and upset that he became at his peers for using it, the more the name stuck, and ultimately Pelé eventually shrugged his shoulders and just accepted the nickname. In a purely coincidental way, perhaps too as a result of growing up with limited funds, Pelé was also unable to afford a real soccer ball. When he was around my same age of six, he would craft a makeshift football, using a rolled up sock stuffed with rags, newspaper, or even fruit, as his ball of choice. Pelé was the most recognizable footballer in the world, and in November of 1969, three months after I was born, he scored his 1,000th career goal. By the time Pelé retired from what he called "the beautiful game" in 1977, he had amassed over 1,200 goals and three FIFA World Cup wins. More than his success and wins on the pitch, Pelé won the hearts of countless numbers of young footballers around the world, including me and my Tunisian mates, all of whom at one time or another had the wind knocked out of our lungs while attempting to recreate his iconic bicycle kick.

When I turned eight, my oldest brother Abdelhanin, bought me a real soccer ball. I was the happiest, luckiest kid in town—no one else had a real soccer ball like mine. When the neighborhood kids heard through the grapevine that I had a real ball, they lined up at my house every evening wanting to play. The main problem? I couldn't always go out to play with them. Remember, when I said I was a natural born salesman? Well, I had an idea to make the best of such a situation, on the evenings I could not go play, I would rent my soccer ball for 2 TND per game. The idea was a hit, everyone loved it, I was able to earn much prized TND, and I started my first business!

Everything with my new firm was going as planned. Fun for my neighborhood pals, and me, when I was able to play. When I was not, "boom!" a few extra TND to tuck into my various hiding spots. One night, however, my brother Moncef took my ball away from the kids during their game and all the kids got upset with *me*! I had to think of a solution quickly and decided to give them their money back—problem solved! They were instantly happy again, and it was one of those first real business lessons learned. I had never heard or seen anyone return money after a purchase, so I'm not sure where the instinct came from. In the moment, we do not know exactly how we will react when tested, and I am glad that my instinct was correct.

An instinct is defined as "a natural or inherent aptitude, an impulse or capacity." My love of gathering money had been tested, and the impulse to be fair won over adding Dinars to my little money box. Or, in this instance, it actually might have been my sock!

As time went by, others in my village started to get their own soccer balls, so business started to decline, along with my collection of TND's. I was ten years old, and unfortunately, my natural skills were not honed to where they are today, which meant that I didn't know that I could innovate or change my strategy at the time. My soccer ball rental business dwindled away, which made me a little sad, but it also provided me with fuel and it was not long before I was on to my next adventure and opportunity!

Take a moment, and reflect back to when you were six to ten years old. Do you remember what you used to love to do? The treasured American writer, Mark Twain once said, "The two most important days in your life are the day you are born and the day you find out why." Clearly, as we can see from my early childhood, I have a natural skill to sell everything, from products to services. Is this why I was born? As we journey through the ensuing chapters, we will be discovering "our *why*" together. I say "our why," because I'm talking about *you* and me in the process. What you may find is that your skills and gifts may also be "your why," specifically you may determine that your why is sales, like me. We can see from my story of my eight-year-old self that sales are not complicated. They don't ever have to be. If you noticed, these were the steps in my first sales journey which can easily be immediately applied, regardless of your gift or why:

1. **Passion!** I loved playing soccer! The thrill of the game, and the camaraderie of playing with neighborhood friends. *What do you love to do?*

   _____

   _____

   _____

   _____

2. **Drive!** I needed to find a way to get a real soccer ball. *What tools do you need? What plans can you make and act upon to figure out how to get them!*

   _____

   _____

   _____

   _____

3. **Implementation!** When I secured my first soccer ball, I started renting it immediately. *What are you able to start, right now? Don't think too much, just start!*

   _____

   _____

   _____

   _____

4. Competition! My customer base began to purchase soccer balls of their own, which meant I was no longer essential for them to have fun. *What changes must you undertake to remain relevant when markets, or conditions, change?*

_____

_____

_____

_____

5. Innovate or Die! My soccer ball rental firm, as a result of changing markets, died. Was that truly what happened? Yes, and no. Yes, in the sense that conditions changed (i.e., demand fell), but I did not adapt to changes. *You choose, innovate or risk closing!*

_____

_____

_____

_____

That's it! My product was a soccer ball. Everyone in my neighborhood loved soccer! I asked for the sale, and my first business venture began. It was a formula of:

- Love the product,
- Get the tools,
- Cherish your client, and
- Ask for the sale!

As a young man, anything I encountered made me think about how I could use it for something else. In other words, I never saw obstacles—only opportunities! I hear the expression today of "think outside of the box" as an *encouragement* to be creative in what you are trying to accomplish. But, *my* reaction when I first heard it was, "What box? Why would I be in a box? There is no box!"

Don't ever put yourself or your thoughts into a box. Just be resourceful![1] Pick up that "soccer ball" that you have in front of you and go for it! Don't underestimate the resources you have around you that you could use or maximize. How can you turn your gift into a skill? The skill then can be something you can sell at the marketplace.

Don't see obstacles![2] Open your eyes and see possibilities. Don't see "No" but how that word leads to a variation of "Yes." Or at least a "Maybe" that will take you to a yes afterwards! Don't complain that you don't have the money to buy this or that—be creative, be smart. Ask questions, be curious. Try to get to know people and always ask for ideas or thoughts about their journeys. Your gift comes from within—those things that excited you and filled you with passion as a child—revisit them and share them with the world!

Don't be ordinary. You and I were born to be extraordinary and to succeed. I asked and asked my way into getting a real soccer ball and rented it out—the only one in my village! Why? We all lacked resources, it was just a matter of having creativity and courage.

The Harvard Business School defines entrepreneurship as, "The pursuit of opportunity beyond the resources currently controlled." Whether you're in a Tunisian schoolyard or Harvard courtyard, I promise you one thing: you *can* find solutions to problems you're passionate about.

Want to know another promise? This journey we're on together is just getting started, and I can't wait to hear where it leads you.

CHAPTER 2
LA BICYCLETTE

 Nothing compares to the simple pleasure of a bike ride.
—*John F. Kennedy*

By ten-years-old, my neighborhood was becoming too small to contain my enthusiasm to explore, thus my fascination with the downtown area of Ain Draham began. I routinely walked the 3 km to downtown where the people were a little different and there were more possibilities to examine. I was in awe! Most of the residents were the owners of all the different businesses in the area and were wealthy. While soccer continued as a favorite childhood sport to play with friends, a new idea began shortly after winding down that first business of mine. One day I saw a boy named Lassad, who was a year older than me, and he had a bicycle! From the moment I saw him ride it around town, I knew I wanted one too. I had to be a little more patient with getting this new "tool" though, since I couldn't just makeshift a bicycle like I did my first home-made soccer ball.

At that point, I was eleven-years-old and my older brothers were still my primary "go-to" investors and were familiar with my repeated requests to purchase a bike. In the meantime, without a homemade option but still wanting to ride, I had heard that Lassad was renting out *his* bicycle downtown. Once I knew that, I would walk 3 km every day to go downtown so I could rent his bike. He charged 2 TND for 100 meters down and 100 meters back. The distance was short because he always wanted to keep an eye on you. Despite the short length of each ride, I very quickly became his best customer. I loved riding that bike and dreaming of how I'd have a bike of my own someday.

In addition to becoming his most loyal customer, I was also his best marketer. I tried to talk anyone into renting his bike so they could see how fun it was to ride. Most of these new kids rejected me at first because they didn't know me since I was from a different neighborhood. I started going to all of the coffeeshops where other kids were hanging out and would start talking to them about what Lassad and I had to offer. The word spread, and we developed new clientele and friendships quickly. Teamwork and collaboration were big lessons from this season as I worked with Lassad and helped him grow his business. It was not because it would later benefit me, but simply because we were good friends.

I enjoyed getting to know these kids that lived downtown a lot —there was just something about them that was different. They seemed to have more opportunities which I admired and was even a little envious of how many more things they had then we did in our neighborhood.

The intrigue about these friends was so great and I loved the downtown area so much that I asked *Ommi* to transfer me to their primary school so I could finish my last two years there with them. None of my neighborhood friends had ever done that. Kids simply went to their nearest school—but I felt like it was where I needed to be to learn more and grow!

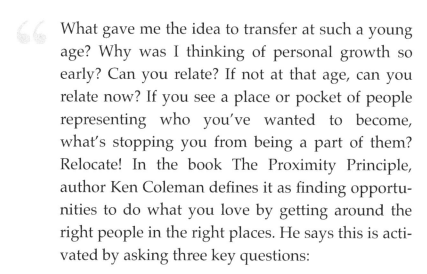 What gave me the idea to transfer at such a young age? Why was I thinking of personal growth so early? Can you relate? If not at that age, can you relate now? If you see a place or pocket of people representing who you've wanted to become, what's stopping you from being a part of them? Relocate! In the book The Proximity Principle, author Ken Coleman defines it as finding opportunities to do what you love by getting around the right people in the right places. He says this is activated by asking three key questions:

1. Who do I need to know?

2. Where do I need to be?

3. What do I need to start doing?

As the waiting list grew to rent Lassad's bike, my new friends and I played games to pass time. My favorite game was chasing each other with flour and eggs. If you got caught, they threw flour all over you so the eggs would stick on you better! I became the fastest kid in the whole group because I didn't want to get caught and get all dirty. I despised the 3 km walk back home to take a shower because I'd miss out on the rest of the game. The slowest kid in the group actually lived right across from where we would play. He got caught all of the time. He was constantly running in and out of his house to wash off to keep playing.

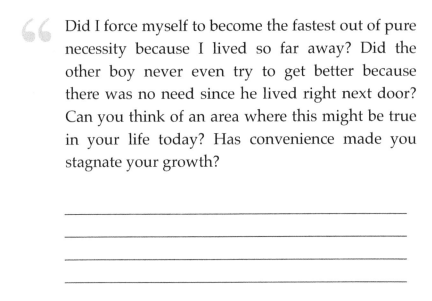

> Did I force myself to become the fastest out of pure necessity because I lived so far away? Did the other boy never even try to get better because there was no need since he lived right next door? Can you think of an area where this might be true in your life today? Has convenience made you stagnate your growth?

As the months passed, Lassad and I grew to be very good friends. He even stopped charging me rent! He now had a second bike of a different size, which meant more opportunities and more customers. I managed the rental of the second one and gave him the money.

However, by the time I was twelve years old, my brother Abdelhanin bought me another life-changing gift: my own bicycle. My family didn't realize I had already learned how to ride since I was riding downtown—nor did they realize how good I had gotten at riding. So they were all very surprised when I hopped on the bike right away!

Within 24 hours of riding, my new bike started falling apart! I cried and thought it was ruined forever. But when my brother saw it, he told me everything just needed to be tightened up. That's what you do with a new bike before riding it, but I didn't know at the time. I was so excited that I just jumped on it and left! I used any tools we had at home or from our neighbors to tighten it back up the best I could.

The next day, I walked it to the city so Lassad could take a look at it and finish fixing it for me. He helped me right away and was so excited for me that I had a brand new bike. Shortly thereafter, I started renting my bike out as well. My prices were 5 TND for 15 minutes or 7 TND for 30 minutes. It was a little harder to start this business up though because the clients weren't lining up outside my house like with my soccer ball. I needed to go to *them* by taking my bike downtown as well. The streets were better to ride there, so that's where the market was. It was a sacrifice, but sales soon increased! Even though Lassad kept renting his bike too, there were plenty of clients for both of us. Because we were friends, our businesses became collaborative rather than competitive with each other. Interestingly, the concept of a shared goal benefiting more than just myself has been a consistent foundation in all of my endeavors, but it started with my friend Lassad.

One time, I accepted an offer for a half-day rental for 12 TND. That price was unheard of. I thought it was a great opportunity until the bike returned broken. It was discouraging at first, but it didn't stop me. I fixed it and continued renting it out. With my profit and my family's assistance, since they were proud of my hard work, I bought myself a second bicycle a few months later—a ten speed bike so I could keep one as a rental and the other for my own riding.

What I learned with my bicycle business was the importance of implementing systems. Lassad and I had our location, time schedule and rental schedule figured out. We also kept watch and good care over our products. In addition to forming our systems, we learned the importance of networking. However, as time went on, the continuous fixing of the bike *did* take a toll on me. It was also a business I could only operate during school vacation and summers since our winters are very harsh in Ain Draham. There were times when the winter snows would accumulate to the point that older homes with aging roofs would collapse under the weight of the snow. Cold winds would follow, freezing water pipes and downing electricity lines for days. Winter days and nights were not as simple as telling Alexa to turn up the thermostat, but *Ommi* kept all of us warm and dry. As a young boy I did my best to help her, and I can vividly recall the bundles of wood, with branches and sticks of various sizes, that she would carry on her back up the hill to the house. She was not only strong mentally, she was physically strong too. In addition to navigating my budding rental business, I was now thirteen-years-old, and entering into secondary school, which meant that school was not only getting harder, but it is when I also experienced a traumatic event.

It was our first year of secondary school. A simple misunderstanding involving a tiny set of nail clippers led my teacher to beat me in front of my classmates and drag me through the school hallways to the Assistant Principal's office. The principal would not believe me, and as punishment he meted out multiple hand lashes—something no child should ever have to experience! I am absolutely certain that the combination of being forcibly removed from my class, and undergoing hand lashing was what led me to sign up for karate classes that had just been announced at our local youth center 5 km away; I never wanted to feel weak or bullied again.

The Bible talks about God turning into good what the enemy intended for evil. That's exactly what that experience of abuse (evil!) and karate as self-defense (good!) became in my life. I fell in love with the sport immediately. Without this experience, I possibly would never have explored karate. I practiced every day and was so obsessed that my brothers told me I would be practicing moves even in my sleep! To this day, karate is deeply ingrained in my core and has never left my side.

تشكيلة الكاراتي بعين دراهم ﴿

Going to the youth center every day to practice karate with the newly formed, first ever karate team in Ain Draham, meant I needed my regular bike for more personal use. Therefore, I didn't have time to rent it out anymore. I had to stop that business as well. Lassad also stopped renting his bikes, but our friendship and love for riding kept growing. We would go to nearby cities at first, and, as we got older and more advanced, we would sometimes ride as much as 50 km a day!

My soccer ball experience was generally positive, so my desire to run another rental business was simply an opportunity to build off the momentum. But even if it had been a bad first experience, my encouragement to you is to try again, and again, and again, and again. Don't worry about your first try that didn't go well. Move on to the next one without assuming it will die too. Don't put yourself or your gift in a box. Don't think, just try again! Don't settle for only opportunities in your neck of the woods either. Aim higher! Look further down the path of what is familiar! Or, if your familiar spot has ran out of ideas, look beyond. Please don't stay in the same spot. Keep progressing and moving forward toward the dream inside you. Keep creating. Keep dreaming. You are unique. No one else has the set of gifts that you have, so go for it. Use them! Remember what Albert Einstein said, "Life is like riding a bicycle. To keep your balance you must keep moving."

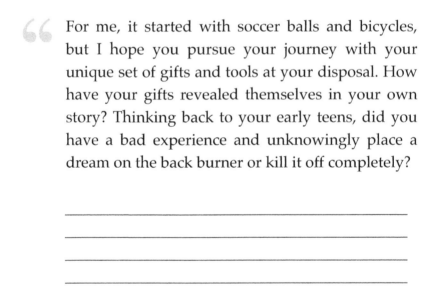

For me, it started with soccer balls and bicycles, but I hope you pursue your journey with your unique set of gifts and tools at your disposal. How have your gifts revealed themselves in your own story? Thinking back to your early teens, did you have a bad experience and unknowingly place a dream on the back burner or kill it off completely?

_____

_____

_____

_____

As with my soccer ball, my bicycle renting business didn't have to be complicated. What I learned from my second venture was that *operating* a business was harder and required a greater sacrifice, even though I instinctively followed the same formula:

1. **Passion!** I loved riding and had to walk 3 km to where I could learn to ride. *Are you willing to sacrifice whatever it takes in order to do what you love?*

    _____

    _____

    _____

    _____

2. **Drive!** I needed to find a way to get a bike and partnered with an existing business. *Are you willing to be at the bottom of an existing business first in order to learn?*

    _____

    _____

    _____

    _____

3. **Implementation!** I started renting my bike immediately because I had learned the ropes. *Do you have the courage to enter a market that has the same offering as you?*

    _____

    _____

    _____

    _____

4. **Competition!** The upkeep of the bike became too much and life's commitments were now competing with my business. *Can you learn the art of delegating in order to avoid burnout?*

_____

_____

_____

_____

5. **Innovate or Die!** In my case again, my bike rental business died. *You'll have the choice of closing or delegating!*

_____

_____

_____

_____

The best part though? Riding the bicycle Einstein speaks of is rent-free. Every day is a chance (and gift!) to ride, and I hope you decide to do so. My bicycle business has stuck with me over the years. One day I heard Jim Rohn say something in his *Best Life Ever* seminar from the early 90's that stuck out to me for obvious reasons:

"I teach kids how to have two bicycles, one to ride, one to rent. Now it doesn't take long to get into business. You don't have to be a genius. Halfway bright, you can start showing a profit."

The day I heard this, it brought tears to my eyes. How true this was for me! I lived it! Yes, it wasn't about having the best or smartest business plan, just about having the courage to ask questions to learn the ropes and execute what you learned. You can start too!

Nabil's Mother (Ommi)

CHAPTER 3
LES LAPINS

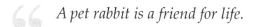 *A pet rabbit is a friend for life.*

Every Monday, the weekly *Souk* in downtown Ain Draham takes place. Souk days are a big deal, as many residents around the city spring to action, mobilizing to go buy or sell.

As early as I can remember, Monday's in Ain Draham were my favorite days. *Ommi's* parents, my grandparents, lived on an olive farm about 20 km away. My *Jaddi* (grandpa) would come riding on his mule or horse every Monday to bring us (depending on the season) fresh olive oil, milk, buttermilk, honey, figs, cherries, olives, apples, oranges, pears, parsley, eggs, homemade breads, etc. One of my favorite all time memories was *Jaddi* riding into town. After visiting with us, he would go to the *Souk* to buy what he needed for the farm, load it, and ride the 20 km home. School vacation was the best of times. Whenever we were on break from school, I loved going to the *Souk* with *Jaddi* or with *Ommi*. It was very exciting with over 4,000 people hustling all over the place. There were always live animals walking around–sheep, cows, chickens, pigeons, you name it, it was there.

In the countries of North Africa, and parts of Western Asia, there are vibrant, active centers of commerce. The word used to describe these areas is *souk*, or souq, which means marketplace.

Originally, and even today, *souks* were an open-air marketplace, typically away from the city center. In general, the *souk* was a place for citizens, merchants and travelers alike to gather to not only conduct trade, but to rest, commune, eat, and shop. In collectivist societies, the *souk* served as the social function mechanism, and they were esteemed to provide a gathering and meeting place for the entire community. For readers that are familiar with grocery store aisles, *souks* are similar in that they are typically divided into sections. Each section represents a different product type, therefore buyers and sellers are effectively aligned from one aisle to the next.

One Monday when I was around fourteen-years-old and at the *Souk* with *Ommi*, I saw a vendor selling rabbits! Rabbits were not common there, so I was surprised and fell instantly in love with their playfulness and cuteness. I asked *Ommi* if we could buy some to have as pets at home. She agreed, so we bought five, two boys and three girls. We had two storage rooms in the back side of our home.

We used one to house the chickens and my plan was to set up my rabbits in the other room. Within a couple of days, I had made little cubbies for each one with brick and cement. I laid out plenty of hay and food for them. I also gathered enough money to buy and build them a fence so they could roam around outside of their room without getting lost or put in danger. I cemented the base of the fence too because they liked to dig and I didn't want them getting out. For me, they were just pure joy to watch and play with! Little did I know what was going to happen next!

Rabbit litters can range in size from 2 to 12 babies called kits. The smaller breeds tend to have smaller litters, and the larger breeds often have more kits per litter. The term for giving birth is called kindling and they can get pregnant again right after having a litter, so you may end up with more rabbits than you know what to do with!

That is exactly what happened! Before I knew it, *Ommi* and I had about 24 rabbits. I knew we were in trouble! I just wanted a handful as pets, and now, we were overflowing with rabbits. I had to think quickly how to solve this problem so I immediately decided to start selling them. It had gotten expensive to care for them as well so I needed to get creative with getting all the feed and hay. I remember noticing several vendors from the *Souk* throwing away their leftover vegetable scraps, like carrot tops and turnips. I asked them to save it for me instead so that I could feed my rabbits. Every Monday, I picked up the scraps after school. I also visited the local restaurants and vegetable shops with which I had made agreements. If they had closed by the time I arrived, they would leave it marked with my nickname *Bulbul* so no one else would take it or throw it away. Sometimes I would have so many food scraps to gather that it would take several bike trips (my own Ford F-150!) to get it all.

I started promoting the sale of rabbits everywhere. I sold them for 8 TND to friends and family, 10 TND to restaurants, and 13 TND to hotels. In addition, I gave away many because they were constantly multiplying! I'll never forget my highest litter too–14 kits! A group of rabbits is called a "fluffle" or a colony. I now had more than 200 rabbits and our business outputs were escalating very fast. Although I enjoyed the rabbits, *Ommi* and I were exhausted with their upkeep. The whole process was too out of control to manage. Even cleaning out their sleeping area was difficult, especially trying to keep it dry during the rains or the snow in the winter. I couldn't sell or give enough of them away either—there were just too many. It was also heart-breaking when some would die in the winter because of the extreme cold, so after two years of caring for the rabbits, it was time to stop.

It was difficult to sell or give away all our rabbits. In my country most locals typically don't eat rabbit, only the foreigners enjoyed them, so it was only the very high-end hotels that would buy them. Finally, after three months, we were able to give our last rabbit away. It was heartbreaking. Even though it had been difficult to keep up with them, especially balancing school and karate in the mix, I loved them very much. I loved racing home from school to watch them play, feed them or count a litter that had just been born. *Ommi* loved them just as much too, especially because she saw the joy they brought to me.

School needed to become my focus since our studies were getting harder and harder. At that time, along with our core subjects, we were studying French, Arabic and English had just been introduced, which was difficult to learn and made me hate the language. Looking back on that now, the irony is not lost on me.

Sometimes, a business opportunity comes knocking at your door without an invitation! All I wanted was to have a handful of pet rabbits. However, a whole new business venture came out of it unplanned. Although it was not my intention when I first saw them, it happened and I jumped on board, instinctively following my same pattern.

1. **Passion!** I loved rabbits and bought a handful to keep as pets. *Would you buy a "pet" just because it brought you pure joy?*

   _____

   _____

   _____

   _____

2. **Drive!** I needed to find a solution to my quickly multiplying pets, fast! *Are you willing to start a business you weren't planning to start?*

   _____

   _____

   _____

   _____

3. **Implementation!** I started asking for help with the feed and finding specific clients interested in buying my rabbits. *Are you willing to be humble and ask for donations and sales?*

_____

_____

_____

_____

4. **Competition!** My "live inventory" superseded my 3 km market radius and I couldn't afford the time commitment to keep going. *Are you willing to be courageous to keep going further and further outside of your market radius until you find a hit?*

_____

_____

_____

_____

5. **Innovate or Die!** In my case, my unexpected rabbit business died. *You'll have the choice of closing or going outside of your borders!*

_____

_____

_____

_____

Did something just stumble into your life that you didn't expect? Don't dismiss it. What if you just bought bunches of beautiful different kinds of flowers and, when you took them home, you realized you were pretty good at arranging them? If the idea pops into your head to start a flower business of some sort, do it! My pet rabbits were like my flowers. I bought them and took them home because they were so beautiful to look at and play with. When they grew into an overflowing garden, a business began.

Starting a business doesn't always have to be intentional—sometimes, it just shows up organically in your journey through life. When it does, you should act on it. Maybe it will lead to something greater, maybe not, but the point is, you tried! Because it was something you *loved*, the experience will be worth it no matter how it ends up. I cherished every moment with my rabbits and I will always love and think fondly of the experience. Don't overthink it. Choosing a venture because it brings you joy is good enough. Remember the box? No? Good, forget about it! There is no box. Enjoy the ride and step into the moment. Anyone that says that "it's just a rabbit," has never loved a rabbit, but whatever your "pet rabbit" is will be your friend for life.

SECTION TWO: ENRICHMENT (BE WILLING TO ADD VALUE; TO YOURSELF AND OTHERS)

DEVELOPING YOUR GIFT

Nabil's Champion, Moncef

CHAPTER 4
IMPOSSIBLE N'EST PAS FRANÇAIS!

 The will to win, the desire to succeed, the urge to reach your full potential . . . these are the keys that will unlock the door to personal excellence. —Confucius

My last two years of secondary school were pretty quiet business-wise. I turned my focus to graduating secondary school and practicing karate. In my country, at the end of your high school years, you have to take a baccalaureate exam if you want to continue in the public higher education system.

Remember my hatred for English? That was the one class I didn't pass. I had to take my last year of secondary school over to pass all of the courses in order to take the baccalaureate. Toward the end of that year, I was swept up in a mutiny by some of the students who lived in the school's dormitories. The students objected to the poor conditions, poor food, and overall their poor treatment. I believe that all of us deserve to be treated with respect, and even though I did support the students, I was wrongfully accused of being part of their protests. Despite the lack of evidence, school leadership decided to expel me from school for eight days.

Upon my return, I was supposed to go to the Assistant Principal's office, the same man who had previously given me lashings five years earlier, along with a family representative. The purpose of the meeting was to be interviewed so I could be allowed to return to school. Part of this interview was to put out my hands to be lashed, in order to prove I was willing to submit to their authority and admit they were correct.

My brother told me to do it, as he was familiar with the Assistant Principal from past business relations, but by that point, I was nineteen-years-old. I already had reached the "black belt" level in karate and was no longer a skinny kid who could easily be bullied. I respectfully refused to put my hands out for lashing. I declared if they weren't willing to let me back in school, I was walking out the door. That's what happened. It was then that I knew my journey was over in Ain Draham. I needed to get out if I wanted to grow. I packed my duffle bag with my karate uniform, two pairs of underwear, pants, shirts, and a bath towel. My sister Samira gave me 40 TND and I set off by bus to the capital city of Tunis.

I planned to find the French Embassy and apply for a Visa. I wanted to explore possibilities to study in France as the next step in my journey. I have loved the French language since I was three years old when my brother, Hafnaoui, taught me the French alphabet. Upon his return from living in France as a young adult, he and others encouraged me in my abilities with the language. I knew a lot of people who had been successful in France as well, so that's where I wanted to go.

But once I had my interview, I realized that was *not* going to be my next step. The visa requirements were unattainable. I needed an invitation letter from someone already living in France, a place to stay while there, a stable life to prove I'd be returning, and ultimately, I was too young, in their opinion, to let me go and trust I would return. However, I didn't walk away from that meeting devastated. It encouraged me to consider my next move—forward, not backward. It may have been an impossibility to go to France at that point, but as the French proverb says, "Impossible is not a French word." In English terms, "There's no such thing as can't." I didn't have to make France happen, but I was going to make *something* happen!

The next nine months were extremely difficult. With my initial 40 TND, 10 TND of which I had already spent enrolling in karate school, I had a lot of things to figure out.

I struggled to find a place to sleep and eat within a city where I was but a small grain of sand. But, I was driven and determined to succeed; I didn't settle for anything less. My strategy was simple: stay curious and ask questions! Remembering my rabbit business when I found myself in uncharted territory, I started asking "How can I" and went out every day with this intention. I would go to the square to meet others and ask things like, "What kind of work do you do? How do you live? Who do you know?" Day-in-and-day-out, I met person after person.

Then one day, I met Moncef who turned out to be from my hometown! Meeting him was my first glimmer of hope in what had become a very dark place. He offered to let me sleep at the studio apartment he and his brother rented and taught me about his work as an *Agent de Transit*.[1]

Everyone I had met up to that point was doing work I was *not* interested in doing. I wanted to work for myself in an industry where there was hope to grow. Moncef taught me everything there was to know about being an *Agent de Transit* and I loved it! He also quickly became my best friend and mentor. *Ommi* was my first Champion, but Moncef was my second true Champion. From the moment we met, he freely gave of himself to help support and guide me, all of which lifted me up and enlightened me.

Even though they weren't hiring more *agents* at Moncef's company, he put me in touch with a company owned by Ayadi. I was hired on the spot! They did not require a degree because they loved my French, my personality and my drive. From that point forward, I made it my mission to be the best *agent* ever!

Depending on your ability as an *agent*, you could be given up to 10 client files to handle in a week. That was me, and I loved it. I knew the ports and the airport like the back of my hand. I built great relationships with the firm's employees and they would take great care of me when I arrived on behalf of our client's imported goods. Sometimes, my clients would meet me directly at the port and, depending on how well and quickly I did my job, they would tip me very nicely! It was a great experience working for Ayadi. I learned from him as he served his clients faster than I did. He came from a town called Sfax where he had gone to school to be an Arabic teacher but after several years, he was not content with the salary or line of work and had moved to the city to find something different.

After two years of working for Ayadi for a monthly salary of 250 TND which I knew was not going to improve, I decided to move towards something else. I intentionally say "moving towards" because my philosophy is not about *leaving* something, but about *moving toward* something in order to continue growing. When I felt it was time to move on, I remembered a company called NGV, Nabli Games & Video, because I frequently saw their products (toys, cassettes, VHS videos, radios, car stereos, etc) coming through customs. I asked them for a *Représentant Commercial* job and they hired me on the spot. For that job, I not only had to have the skills of an *agent*, but also had to have a license and know how to drive!

Back then, you couldn't apply for a driver's license until you were twenty years old. It was quite the process. You would first take driving lessons, and after a while, when the teacher felt you were ready, you would go to a Government office for a test. The government officer would pass you or not, based on your driving skills, personality, and unfortunately, at times, the amount of your bribe. When I first inquired about the process, I was told to not even try because of the difficulty and expense. What they didn't know was that I already knew how to drive so it wasn't going to take me long. I learned to drive at eighteen from my older cousin, Nouredine, who worked as a car mechanic in his hometown of Baboush 5 km away. I got to practice on all of his cars and became very good at it!

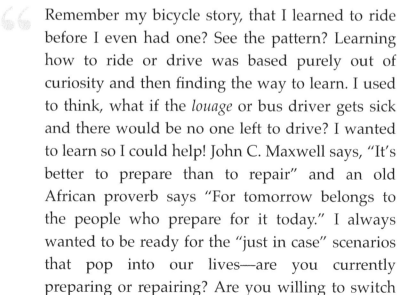

Remember my bicycle story, that I learned to ride before I even had one? See the pattern? Learning how to ride or drive was based purely out of curiosity and then finding the way to learn. I used to think, what if the *louage* or bus driver gets sick and there would be no one left to drive? I wanted to learn so I could help! John C. Maxwell says, "It's better to prepare than to repair" and an old African proverb says "For tomorrow belongs to the people who prepare for it today." I always wanted to be ready for the "just in case" scenarios that pop into our lives—are you currently preparing or repairing? Are you willing to switch your pattern if you tend to constantly be in repair-mode?

_____

_____

_____

_____

_____

_____

_____

_____

I went to an agency to get some hours of driving so they'd recommend me for a license. I was able to get recommended after 20 hours of driving, as opposed to the typical 60+ hours it normally took. I easily passed the test and became the proud owner of a driver's license. I did not have a car, and owning a car anytime soon was out of the question, but still, I had a drivers license, and therefore, I had possibilities! In no time at all, because I had gone through the process of obtaining my license, I was able to get my second job in the city which paid me 350 TND per month with NGV.

I loved my job at NGV. I wasn't just driving across the city but throughout the whole country of Tunisia as I delivered products to our customers. As soon as my company truck was loaded every morning, the clock began ticking for everything to be delivered on time. Traffic was absolutely insane, so I became razor sharp in my driving skills—meeting my goals no matter what, even when I encountered a herd of cows and after one had gotten so scared, it came charging at my truck and pierced its head through my driver's side window that thankfully I had open! Only the karate instincts I had acquired up until that point saved me from being severely injured, as I quickly maneuvered my body to get out of the way, and then have the courage to push its head back out!. During my three years with NGV, my driving record was not exactly spotless.

Counting NGV Receivables for the Day

Perhaps due to taking risks and my desire to reach my goals, I had my share of speeding tickets and fender benders; however, I was NGV's best sales and collections representative despite having the most difficult territory. After three years, I grew weary from the hustle and grind.

Many days it would take fifteen hours to finish the route, and after a serious car accident, I began to feel it was time to move towards the next step in my life.

I did not know exactly where I would move to next, and although I wasn't in business for "myself" in the city, you can see that my strategy stayed consistent from my childhood:

1. **Passion!** I loved growth and was going to go where it was at. *Where is your next step in growth located? Are you on a "bus" heading there yet?*

_____

_____

_____

_____

2. **Drive!** I needed to find a solution to my failed first attempt at growth, fast! *Are you willing to keep trying even after failed Plans A, B, C, D...?*

_____

_____

_____

_____

3. **Implementation!** I excelled at my first job and got my license without having a need for it. *Are you willing to do what it takes to be the best in your position? Are you willing to continue growing your toolbelt without having a reason for certain tools, yet?*

_____

_____

_____

_____

4. **Competition!** The path I was on came to an end; time for growing pains again on this competition of life. *Are you willing to welcome growing pains in your life?*

_____

_____

_____

_____

5. **Innovate or Die!** I kept choosing to move towards growth, rebirthing myself. *You'll have the choice to go back, staying stagnant, or moving towards growth! Which one will it be?*

_____

_____

_____

One night, after a particularly long day, I headed back to the NGV office to drop off my collections from the day. I entered the office, and as I began to walk up the stairs I heard a low, muffled voice. When I reached the hallway at the top of the stairs and turned, the voice I heard was one of the co-owners, Mustafa. He was speaking in English on a phone call with a client. Right then, something happened inside of me. For the first time in my life, I felt like the English language was important. There was something powerful about the language when it came to business. I realized if I wanted to continue growing in my career, I needed to learn English. In that instant, a light switch went off and I heard an almost audible voice say to me what has become a life changing, most important phrase, "learn English, it will take you somewhere!"

Nabil's Champion, John

CHAPTER 5
"LEARN ENGLISH, IT WILL TAKE YOU SOMEWHERE!"

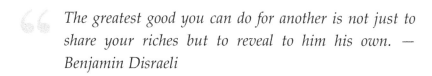

The greatest good you can do for another is not just to share your riches but to reveal to him his own. —Benjamin Disraeli

NGV, where I worked in Tunis, had a showroom on the Avenue de la Liberté, the same street where just a block away was the language school IBLV (Institut Bourguiba des Langues Vivantes). This area was filled with activity, and often, after leaving the showroom from dropping off merchandise, if I had some extra time, I would go to the coffeeshop down the street facing the school. I remember noticing the international students coming and going and it piqued my interests about them and their studies.

IBLV

During these times, while watching the bustling students, the pull to move towards something different was strong. At this point in my journey with NGV, I was ready, so I researched the school's English language program. It was a four-year degree. However, they had an intensive option of going to class four hours a day. It would be hard, for certain, but I *knew* that was my next step. I didn't have the mental capacity or time to go to night school and keep working. So, I had a choice to make: keep my job or resign and pursue where learning English would take me.

I chose to move forward and pursue English language studies in order to reach this "somewhere." I had plenty of money saved up and, by that point, was sharing an apartment with three other roommates so my contribution towards rent was very manageable. My last day at NGV was filled with well wishes and I started the intensive program right away. I was still uneasy with the English language, but because I knew I needed it in order to keep growing, I became obsessed with it. I went to class four hours per day and then spent my evenings studying, sometimes getting so frustrated that I would throw the dictionaries to the wall, and walk away, only to come back again because of that nudge inside of me saying that "I was going somewhere." It felt like something bigger and more powerful was taking place inside of me and driving me to keep studying and preparing. It would later turn into a beautiful love story with the language. Classwork was only one part, I needed to practice with native speakers as well. I missed my family, and the camaraderie, and the feelings of the ties that bind. In this way, the perfect scenario would be to meet a family whom I could befriend and practice English. I had asked the administration about this and they said they couldn't help and to ask the professors—I asked them, who in turn said they couldn't help me either.

One Monday morning, as I was entering the coffee shop before my 8am class, I ran into a tall Westerner at the door who had just received his coffee and had turned around to walk out. He smiled at me and said *"Sabah el kheir"* which completely shocked me! I smiled back at him, said "Good Morning" and we continued to speak while walking—this man, named John, with his limited Arabic, and me with my limited English. We both ended up at the language school and told each other, "Here, noon, today."

As I walked out of my class at noon, there was John, waiting for me, with his wife and two small children with him. They were the family I had hoped to meet and practice English with! It was the start of another beautiful friendship that came straight from living in the city. John and his family were from South Carolina and had only been in the country for about a month studying Arabic. I was able to help them. I took John to the local market to teach him the vocabulary for fruits and vegetables and in turn, he taught me the vocabulary for all of those words in English! John and I would meet almost every morning for coffee or have lunch together and I spent time in their city home almost weekly. John, too, became a true Champion for me, always selflessly helping and encouraging me to get better.

After graduating, in June of 1994, at twenty-five years of age, with perfect scores in my intensive course, I decided to go through the two-year *Force du Vente* program at the *École de Commerce* which was conducted in English, French, and Arabic. This program was sponsored by the Tunisian Chamber of Commerce. Joining it meant another two years without working full-time and my savings were not going to sustain the cost. My sister, Samira, supported me again. She became another Champion to bless me in my life. I wouldn't have made it through that season without her. She always loved and helped *Ommi* in raising me and after my move to the city, she often supported me financially when I wasn't able to do so myself.

I loved my program at the Chamber of Commerce. Through my time with them, I applied and was accepted into a six-month unpaid internship with TunisAir. As an intern, I got to meet everyone in the company. My role was to interview employees and write about their roles. I was like a "fly on the wall" so to speak. With no specific role to fulfill for the company—I simply got to observe, learn, and write about the business. I saw employees on their best and worst days. This was an experience I highly value to this day with my own company. I have a strong personal desire for our employees' well-being through a safe and positive work environment.

During this period, John introduced me to his Korean friend, Mr. Kim. He was living in our city with his family and I established a nice relationship with him. He told me about Mr. Ryou, the General Manager of Samsung Corporation's bridges and heavy industry division, who had just arrived in Tunisia seeking to establish the country's first local office. He needed someone to open the office for him and Mr. Kim asked if I'd like to meet him since he knew I was in the last leg of my *Force du Vente* program. I said, "Of course!" This led to my first job interview, all in English! Once Mr. Ryou heard of my job and educational experience, he realized I aligned perfectly with the needs of this new office. He offered me a job as the Office Manager with my own personal secretary. The job included a 550 USD monthly salary, the most anyone in my family, friends, or hometown ever made! Plus the right to use the company car, a brand new burgundy BMW 540i sedan, whenever I needed it! So here it was, English had just taken me to my first "somewhere"!

I couldn't have made it this far in the city alone. Laura Gassner Otting, of Limitless Possibility, eloquently affirms that "...champions. Oh, champions invite you to opportunities, they put your name into consideration, they open doors. They take an active role in helping you make things happen." My Tunisian friend, Moncef, was my first non-blood related Champion and mentor. He took me in, got to know me and started showing me the ropes right away. He was there for me no matter what. He never held back any information or advice that he felt could help me. He shared his meals, his finances and his support. Even after I moved out, he continued to check in with me. He met me for coffee weekly, sometimes even without scheduling it because we knew each other's paths so well, and gave me constant encouragement. "You can do this, Nabil!" We spent many hours together both laughing and crying. He'll forever be in my heart. Without him, I wouldn't have had my first breakthrough into the city with my first great job or even my second job that followed.

My American friend, John, was my second Champion as well as a father figure. He encouraged me, called me, invited me over, gave me advice and cheered for me on the journey. He was the definition of a "father to the fatherless" and for someone who never got to have these conversations with his own father, I am forever grateful for his investment in my life. I knew I could rely on him and that he would drop everything to support me. The most important things he taught me were by his actions. He treated his family and those around him with love and respect. What a great legacy for me to share with others! Without him, I wouldn't have gotten a job with

Samsung Corporation, which was the best opportunity and job offer in my life up to that point.

———

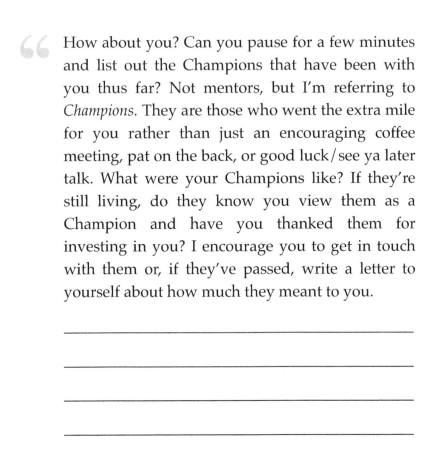

How about you? Can you pause for a few minutes and list out the Champions that have been with you thus far? Not mentors, but I'm referring to *Champions*. They are those who went the extra mile for you rather than just an encouraging coffee meeting, pat on the back, or good luck/see ya later talk. What were your Champions like? If they're still living, do they know you view them as a Champion and have you thanked them for investing in you? I encourage you to get in touch with them or, if they've passed, write a letter to yourself about how much they meant to you.

_____

_____

_____

_____

———

If you haven't had a Champion in your life, no worries. A person like that *will* come. Just keep putting yourself out there! Entrepreneur.com says, "So how do you get started finding a champion? You don't. A champion finds you. They see the fire in your belly and the determination in your eyes. They've seen you perform, fail and keep trying. They know they can take a personal risk, because they know you will not let them down."

So don't go through life hiding from a corner. Speak up, be known, be heard, be understood. The right person, at the right time, *will* be listening and want to champion you to the next level. In turn, is there someone *you* can champion along their journey? It's best to always look both ways to see who's coming up behind you and who has gone before you.

CHAPTER 6
THE ONE WHO KEPT REHEATING HIS FOOD

 To have another language is to possess a second soul.
—Charlemagne

B y the time I was twenty-eight years old and working with Samsung Corporation, I felt great! I was working with a company I loved and doing things at which I excelled. I was also an English interpreter for my new boss, Mr. Ryou, at all of our business meetings with Tunisian officials, attorneys, CPA's and foreign clients, which was completely new for me! I never thought of interpreting as part of any career or being a career in itself, besides at the UN. It was extremely gratifying to see how needed my language services in Arabic, French and English were. Hotel staff workers (where we held these business meetings for Samsung) knew I'd always need my food reheated since I never had time to eat the meals as soon as they came out since I was interpreting back and forth for everyone!

About a year into working with Samsung, I felt a sharp pain in my stomach. I called a taxi for the nearest clinic. Once I got there, they let me know I needed an emergency surgery to remove my gallbladder. What a shock! I called Mr. Ryou to let him know I probably wouldn't be able to open the office on Monday. He visited me at the clinic the very next day and told me he was going to cover my hospital bill. The total bill represented a three month salary for me. I was speechless at his generosity.

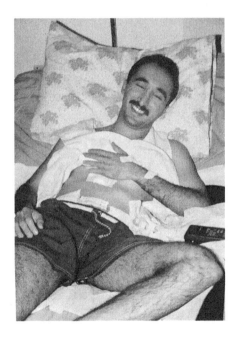

I told him I could repay him over time, but he refused to take my money. Mr. Ryou's kindness showed me he cared about me as a person and not just an employee. Over the last year of working together, he had seen my dedication. He knew I often worked all hours of the day or night based on what was needed (sometimes we had to stay at the port from 8am-

10pm!). Our relationship had become more like family than friends. He often took me to dinner if we'd had a long night of work and we would talk about the difficult aspects of business and the sacrifice it required. I enjoyed my work, especially because my dedication was noticed and appreciated. What an incredible gesture on his part, a man of incredible work ethic that I will never forget!

Shortly after my hospital stay, Mr. Ryou decided it was time to retire, and Mr. Choi was his replacement. He was another incredible boss. As time passed and through my continued relationship with John and his family, I met another American couple visiting Tunisia, Charles and Kristy. We became good friends and they invited me to their home state of Kansas for a visit. By mid-1999, business had slowed down quite a bit in our Samsung office so I felt it was a good time to ask if I could travel. Mr. Choi not only accepted my leaving for a month, but he gave me a wonderful gift–*paid* leave. My visa interview went perfectly and I was approved for 30 days of travel. Everything seemed to line up and I was off to Kansas!

I flew directly from Tunis to Frankfurt and then on to the United States. When I arrived at O'Hare Airport in Chicago for my layover, I was extremely overwhelmed. The airport was so big and there were people everywhere! I was hungry and only had a few US dollars in my pocket. I ordered the cheapest item on the menu in front of me: a hot dog. I couldn't believe they ate "dog meat" in America. I asked the server if it was truly dog meat since it was my first time in the country. She laughed hysterically and explained to me what was in it. I ended up buying two hot dogs and quickly became a fan. I did not know it at the time, but Americans love hotdogs. According to the National Hot Dog and Sausage Council, we purchase nine billion every year from grocery stores! The two I bought and ate were delicious, and after that, I found my gate for Kansas City and was off to my final destination. Charles and Kristy were waiting for me at the airport with their kids. It was then my American adventures began!

The great film director Victor Fleming never mentioned during his filming of The Wizard of Oz where exactly in Kansas the character Dorothy hailed. Perhaps this was intentional, or he felt it unnecessary. Regardless, my visit to Kansas took me through a cultural immersion tornado that I can still feel to this day. In many ways it was indescribable, and I absolutely knew I wasn't in Tunisia anymore! The family had arranged an incredible month for me to experience all kinds of people and activities to give me a complete cultural experience. The plan was for me to move to a different home every two to three days. The idea was great, but it proved to be exhausting. The whole process of getting to know host families and answering all of their questions about who I was and where I came from would start over every few days. I truly experienced American life through so many homes, meals, confusing types of shower knobs, conversations, family structures, and it was all so new and exciting. It was my first time being completely surrounded by English from every direction! It was an enormous change for me, everything was so different. The construction and direction of streets, subdivisions, schools, churches, restaurants and coffee shops were all a new experience. Especially the coffee shops! Back home, coffee shops are our main gathering place and part of our everyday lives, but here they were so different - they were so organized and no one was talking to each other! My approach became "just make it through the day" as I absorbed everything and tried to keep up with each conversation.

I had a lot of emotions to process when the month was over and it was time for me to return home. I can't put into words exactly how I felt, except for the feeling of another nudge that this was somehow part of my "going somewhere" and I felt like I'd be back.

I flew from Kansas City to Chicago, and after another layover at O'Hare where I added a few more hotdogs to the annual per capita sold, I landed back in Tunis. It was full speed ahead with the life I had left behind a month ago, but now I returned with a much sharper English-speaking ability! My job with Samsung Corporation continued to absorb most of my time and energy, but about six months after my trip to Kansas, things started to change within our division. The market had been steadily slowing down for us in Tunisia as our country was not interested in importing our large machinery, but it was steadily picking up in Libya! The Tunisian market was more prone to do business with the European market, whereas Libya was doing more business with the Asian market. Mr. Choi was now spending more time in Libya than he was in our home office and eventually asked whether I'd be willing to relocate permanently when he closed the Tunisian office. I agreed to test it out for a month and helped with the liquidation and closure of our office. After moving, I lived in a company apartment rent-free above the Libyan office. My salary jumped to 750 USD a month and I got my own company car–a brand new silver Volvo S60 sedan! On paper, everything seemed like it should have worked out. I was taking a very natural next step in my career and I had full support all around me so it seemed like all systems were "Go." But I felt like something was off in my gut.

Where had my entrepreneurial spirit and drive gone? I loved working for Samsung and had two great bosses thus far. But it wasn't my *personal* business I was running, it was theirs. I felt that I was losing my edge and not being stimulated on a daily basis anymore. Work had become routine and monotonous. It was a wonderful, stable, nice job, but as an entrepreneur, I was growing antsy. I wanted to hustle, to meet new people every day, to get back to buying and selling, to making profits. Jim Rohn says "Work hard at your job and you can make a living. Work hard on yourself and you can make a fortune." This describes the difference between an employee and an entrepreneur. I had filled an employee role over the last decade and had learned so much about business from some very great examples but was longing to figure out my own start-up by this point.

Indeed.com defines the following two words:

- **Employee**: Employment is the act of working *for* a company to receive compensation in return. Companies build a workforce by hiring professionals to fill certain roles and complete tasks that can benefit the business.
- **Entrepreneur**: Entrepreneurship is the act of starting a business to make it profitable. The business owner makes the proper investment to control the operations and they spearhead the services the business provides.

One is not better than the other, it's just a matter of which one you are and whether you're following that path!

All of these unsettling feelings, coupled with being in a foreign country without any friends or family, were not a good formula for me. I knew the time had come where I needed to move toward something else. I let Mr. Choi know after working there twenty-one days that the position in Libya was not for me. He was very understanding and accepted my resignation kindly. He even offered me a 2,500 USD severance check. I headed back *home* at that point, back to my roots in Ain Draham, to recalibrate and figure out my next step in life.

 Where do you find yourself today? Are you in the right role? Are you following your gut too? If you're not in the right role, change it. Do something about it. You've probably been riding it out for a while and if it's not going to change or satisfy your creativity, it's not going to bring you true joy. You don't have enough years to keep wasting; if the journey you're on is not you, leave it. Yes, it's risky to leave, especially if too much time has passed and it has become a comfort zone. But it's worth moving towards the next step in order to take a chance on your happiness. It's like a dance, the beat to the specific rhythm that wants to play out in your life and is inviting you to follow it. The way I see it, the bigger risk in life is spending years dancing to a beat you weren't meant to follow. If you have the entrepreneurial spirit, chase it, go after it, sacrifice for it. It's who you are. So go home, but go all the way back *home*, and recalibrate!

My three years at Samsung Corporation had come to an end. The experiences that I had, professionally and personally, were incredible and they allowed me to meet and have great adventures and encounters with amazing people. At the end of the day, I was being pulled towards something more, and I knew that I needed to follow my gut, wherever that might take me.

SECTION THREE: FAIRNESS (BE HONEST; WITH YOURSELF AND OTHERS)

MAXIMIZING YOUR GIFTS

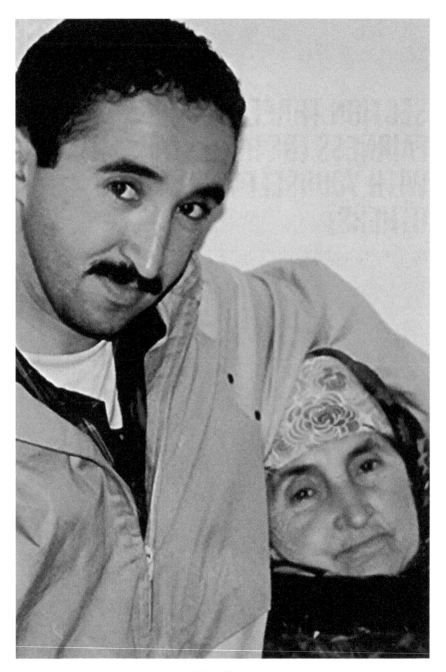

Going Home

CHAPTER 7
WHAT IS YOUR FOUR-YEAR PLAN?

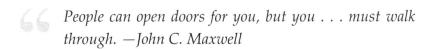 *People can open doors for you, but you . . . must walk through.* —*John C. Maxwell*

The idea of going home has a number of possible connotations, but when I refer to "going home to recalibrate" I mean figuratively since the physical representation of *home* may no longer exist, or eventually will no longer exist. I'm blessed to still be able to spend time with *Ommi*, the safest person from my roots. In this way, "going home" means going back to her, and to the physical hearth and home, and the mountain where I was raised.

What is your earliest memory of your safest place or person? Please take time to process where or who that might be so you know where to go when you need to recalibrate. If you can't go physically, set up some sort of marker in representation of that place or person for you and put it up where you can refer to it often to go back to your true north.

I had returned from my trip to the United States, Libya, and Tunis, and I was back home in Ain Draham. Internally, I was at a crossroads. I was thirty years old, and I did not have a clear path towards my next opportunity. The only thing that I knew was that I was going to pave something out, and fast. Fast in its adjective form means "to be firmly fixed." Success was what I desired to be affixed to, and I needed to figure out where it was taking me next. Remember how I defined success back in Chapter One? It's living out a life in the sweet spot of what you love and what you're gifted to do. In a speech, John C. Maxwell said, "The secret of my success, if there is any success at all, is that I love what I do." I wasn't there yet.

One night, I was reflecting on my trip to America, and I distinctly remembered the gut feeling I had when I left the U.S., that I would return one day. The following day, I decided to follow through with the idea of returning to America. During my first trip, one of the many families that had hosted me during my month-long visit had introduced me to an educator named Greg. My host family had set up a time for me to go to Greg's school to share with his students. It was an opportunity to talk about where I was from and to answer students' questions. The entire experience was unforgettable. Not the least of which were the students' notions of what I looked like! Based on their overall impressions of Africans, they assumed I would be a tall, strong, black man wearing traditional clothing! When I got in front of them as a white man with thinning hair and wearing a polo, they were surprised. I was not wearing traditional clothing either; the only thing traditional about me was my way of greeting each other, men or women, with a kiss on each cheek. After I explained it, and Charles and I demonstrated it, still no one wanted to practice our greeting—not even Greg! All in all it was an enlightening experience, and I enjoyed the time that I spent with Greg and his students.

Greg and I had a great conversation on our way back to his house, with a very genuine connection, and was the person that I reached out to to ask if he'd write me a letter of invitation. Upon receiving my request, Greg was thrilled I had reached out, and he gladly agreed to write an invitation letter for me. As I waited for the letter, I gathered the necessary travel documents and embassy requirements to submit for my visa. I was once again approved, this time for a six month visa! A door had opened for me and I was going to walk, and in short order, fly through it.

The pursuit of success can become more difficult as you age. Why, you might ask? It is a natural progression to have more voices, both internal and external, that oppose and tempt you to "just settle down, it's much easier that way!" Doing so was not an option for me, but it did not make my decision to return to the United States any easier, and frankly I was unprepared for how close this next step was going to hit home to *Ommi*.

"The only outbound flight to Kansas City is Thursday, March 16," the travel agent told me. The year was 2000, but what is the significance of March 16? This is the exact date of Eid al-Adha. As defined by the History Channel, the celebration of "Eid al-Adha" or the "Feast of Sacrifice," signifies the willingness of the Prophet Ibrahim, known as Abraham in Christianity and Judaism, to sacrifice his son, Ismail as ordered by Allah. It is one of Islam's most important holidays. Usually lasting three to four days, and celebrated by millions of Muslims worldwide, the holiday begins on the 10th day of the Muslim calendar lunar month of Dhul-Hijja, at the time of Hajj, the annual pilgrimage to Mecca. Considered the holiest of the two Eids, the other being Eid al-Fitr, or "Festival of Breaking the Fast," that commemorates the end of Ramadan, it is one of two major Muslim holidays celebrated across the globe each year.

Eid al-Adha is not a quiet, or somber celebration, and for Ommi it is meaningful and significant. As a widow, she expected the whole family to travel *home* to be together and celebrate the sacrifice of the lamb. The purchase of a lamb was something we saved up for all year long and it was so joyful to purchase our own animal as a family unit.

On the actual day of Eid al-Adha, an elder is appointed to kill and butcher it. The sacrifice is not about shedding blood for God, but rather it is about giving up something held dear in devotion. It is also a means of helping to feed the poor, as a portion of the lamb is offered and saved for them while the rest is cooked for the family feast later that day. Eid al-Adha is a culmination point within the year and it was *my* favorite time of year too. There is nothing like being reunited and enjoying a meal together, especially the delicious liver!

But this year, my seat at *Ommi's* table would be empty. For the first time in my thirty years of age, her last-born would not be present. Knowing that we would not be together, we were both sad the day of my departure. After breakfast, as I gathered my bags for my trip and prepared to walk out through our front door, *Ommi*, with tears streaming, said, "Go, live up to the meaning of your name." In the Arabic language, my name means noble. *Ommi* was proud to have given me my name and I hoped to do as she instructed me. As I settled into my seat on a packed airliner destined for Kansas City, *Ommi's* words whispered within my mind, just as they do now, "Go, live up to the meaning of your name."

Looking back, I see that on this particular day her sacrifice was offering up her beloved son. She was able to live out Eid al-Adha in a very real way this year, giving me up without knowing if she'd ever see me again. She is the strongest woman I have ever met and will always be my hero.

 When your next step involves a deep sacrifice, have you found yourself backing away? We'd like growth to only be hard and painful on *us* individually but it sometimes takes casualties of those around us. We're tempted to obey the voice telling us to "just settle down." But then again, you'll never know what it could have looked like if you had taken a painful step towards growth. *Ommi's heart was broken, but she knew I was in pursuit of my "somewhere."* Don't be afraid of the pain. It will take your breath away, but it's only temporary!

As we were descending on O'Hare for my layover, I was stunned to see the Chicago River had turned an iridescent green! It was now March 17th - St. Patrick's Day! Once inside and in line for my new tradition of buying a hot dog, I noticed the people were all dressed in green too! What was going on? I did not understand, but everyone seemed to be in a celebratory mood and it made me feel invigorated too! I was even more confused when I landed in Kansas City because my host family, who had arrived to meet me at the terminal, were also dressed in green! Chicago, which ties with New York City, has the first and second largest St. Patrick's Day Parade celebration. I now know that Kansas City is the third largest in the United States, possibly due to the fact that Kansas City was largely built by Irish immigrants. My host family explained the traditions of the day, and I felt that having a little Luck O' the Irish was not a bad way to kick off my next six months in America!

 Fun Fact: The meaning of my Arabic name, Nabil, means *noble* and the English equivalent is Patrick, meaning *nobleman*! Wikipedia confirms this stating, "The name Nabil has a similar meaning to the

English given name Patrick." What are the odds? Coincidence sure, but a fun one! I didn't know this at the time, but knowing it now gives me a little extra confirmation I made the right decision that day to take the flight to America—whether I'm a saint or not!

The contacts that I had made during my previous whirlwind trip were numerous. I had met Bill and Steve over a lunch and now, they happened to be eating at the same restaurant Charles and I had just stopped in for a bite to eat. We reconnected and ended up having a great conversation about life and goals. One of my first goals on this trip was to contact Bill again and ask if he could take me to visit a school that he had mentioned to me previously. The school amongst other subjects was well known for its curriculum which taught about God and life's meaning. I was interested in inquiring about applying to be a student. School was always a safe environment for me to assess and reevaluate myself; process, learn and consider my next steps. It gave way to open doors to begin something new. Bill was happy to arrange a visit and picked me up in his red, two-door Ford Ranger pick-up truck. I remember this day vividly. I was feeling extremely optimistic and encouraged.

As part of my visit to the school, I was scheduled to speak in a classroom to talk about my dreams and goals. I was nervous, but excited for the opportunity as well. I was still an English learner and now I was giving a speech and being interviewed in front of the school's faculty. The questions posed were weighty, one after another, landing with the thud of a medicine ball. I was asked about my plans after graduation. What was I going to do with my degree? How would I serve? Where would I live once I was finished? The questions got harder and harder. The problem was, I didn't have the answers they were looking for. I was thirty years old, but felt like a two-year-old child repeatedly answering, "I don't know." The truth was, I didn't even know what I was going to do the very next day, let alone four years from then! The final question was the one that was the heaviest, "How are you going to pay for the program?" What? I literally thought it was free to learn about God. When I asked the price, the reply was 50,000 USD! I knew the door was closed. My time with them ended, there were promises to look into the visa process for international students, but I foresaw what eventually did, or more appropriately didn't happen—we never spoke to each other again. Now what?

My first days back in America were not as expected, I felt overwhelmed and the voice inside of me was telling me that it was best to return to Tunisia. America was just too big and too expensive! When we arrived back at Bill's house, Steve was there waiting to invite me to dinner at his home. I was so exhausted by that point, I just got in his car and left. We ate homemade spaghetti, salad, bread and talked until midnight. Steve encouraged me to ride out my visa by exploring other possible doors while living in their basement. Sometime in the predawn hours, the voice telling me to return home, switched to telling me to accept Steve's generous offer.

Steve encouraged me to begin nearby at Johnson County Community College. I liked the sound of that—it reminded me of an old advertisement I had seen years ago about community colleges in America and loved the concept, assuming it meant community as I understood it to mean! His wife helped me apply. I found a sponsor, and within eleven days, my visa status from tourist to student was approved. This process usually takes 120-180 days. Why was mine approved in eleven days? I needed this little miracle, and once again, I was a student.

Community colleges are a hidden secret. In the case of Johnson County Community College, it is not so hidden, because it is well supported by the community. Community colleges provide a place for traditional and nontraditional students, which are all those that may be older or returning to college after a significant time away. One of the other factors that permeates community colleges are the significant numbers of diverse cultures served by the college, with English Language Learners (ELL) being one of them. My English was tested before starting my program and to my surprise, I received high enough scores that I didn't need to enroll in ESL (English as a Second Language) classes! Another miracle.

I still had more hurdles to go through to start school. I paid the international student tuition with the 900 USD left from my severance check, but nothing remained for books. Two weeks into the semester and I still hadn't found a solution. How could I pay for it all? I felt again like it was best to return to Tunisia. Nevertheless, I let go of my pride and went to speak with the Dean of International Students.

He assured me there was a grace period option for international students and gave me the choice of a free semester either at the beginning or the end of the program. When I heard these words, I cried visible tears. This was my third little miracle. The stress I had been carrying had become so great that only my tears could release the pressure. I chose to apply this "option for grace" to my first semester and the college returned my tuition right away. I bought some food first since I was starving, then went to buy my books at the campus bookstore. I finally felt my legs under me enough to get me started on my American educational journey. Looking back, I'm not sure this *grace option* was really true, or was God himself offering me His grace through the Dean to encourage me to keep going? If so, it was another much needed miracle and another step towards my "somewhere."

I suppose it's ironic that I landed in America, in pursuit of my next step, awash in a sea of green. Green, the color of money, and money is how it all began! I could not pay for my first choice of school so that was a closed door and I almost had to withdraw from my second choice because, even though the program was more manageable, I couldn't pay for the books. America is the land of opportunity, yes, but it's not just handed to you at your port of entry. I was no longer fishing in my Mediterranean Sea, this was now a much bigger ocean and much farther away from being able to just go *home*. I began to feel that the adhesive that I used to hold fast to success was weakening, and the added language and cultural barriers were not helping me to adhere. The voice that whispers to us in the dead of night, or while we are walking alone through the college campus, telling us to just settle was definitely tempting at this point. But, I continued to follow the footsteps of my foundational years:

1. **Passion!** I wanted to follow the path, even if it meant moving overseas, where growth opportunities existed. *Write out a growth opportunity and its location that you have been ignoring.*

————————————————————————

————————————————————————

————————————————————————

————————————————————————

2. Drive! I pursued contacts and resources to assist me in this step. *Next, write down the contacts needed to help you achieve this growth opportunity, and contact them!*

_____

_____

_____

_____

3. Implementation! I made the most difficult decision in my life at that point, and left. *What is it going to take to implement this? Are you willing to count the cost for the sake of your journey towards growth?*

_____

_____

_____

_____

Don't ever shy away from trying either, because just as my student visa was approved in a tenth of the time of the "normal" process, your opportunity could unexpectedly be just around the corner too! Are you willing to still try?

_____

_____

_____

4. **Competition!** You need money, you need money, you need money. *Once the price tag pops up, we feel hopeless and have the tendency to back away. How much is your growth opportunity going to cost you? Write it down and make a plan for obtaining it.*

_____

_____

_____

_____

5. **Innovate or Die!** My grace option gave me the green light to keep moving forward. *I was embarrassed to tell anyone that I didn't have enough money for books, but as soon as I did, the scholarship offer came my way. Is your pride keeping you from sharing your needs? Once you're willing to share, you will be surprised how many people want to genuinely support you along your journey towards growth!*

_____

_____

_____

_____

Our journeys can become more complex, and they can get harder as we follow our "somewhere," but the life lessons, learnings, and tools we acquire along the way can help us through. The more we access them from our toolbelt, the better we become at utilizing them. *Ommi* once told me, "God says I will give my hard work to the person who can carry it, who can handle it. He gave you strength and ability. Rely on God, He will be with you and be your defender." You *can* do the hard thing. Don't give up on your growth. Continue your next step even if you don't know your full "four year plan!"

CHAPTER 8
ME VS. IMMIGRATION, FINAL SCORE?

 I learned that courage was not the absence of fear, but the triumph over it. The brave man is not he who does not feel afraid, but he who conquers that fear. —Nelson Mandela

As a newly inducted college student in America, my visa limited my ability to work to a maximum of twenty hours a week on campus. Since I was still practicing karate, I applied to work at the college gym. I was hired to cover the morning shift on weekdays.

Every day, I opened the gym by 5am, worked, went to class, did homework, practiced karate, and started it all over again the next day!

I did this for two years, but a year into this schedule, I needed to move closer to school and my only financial option was moving into an empty room at Steve's church.

Living alone in a building was a new experience but I accepted the challenge. The HVAC system was on a timed program, and I was not allowed to change the temperature settings, which meant it would get very cold at night. I harnessed my creativity to keep warm. I would iron my sheets to reach the maximum temperature of "just before scorching," then quickly put them and all of my clothes over me. I also needed to get creative in other areas, so I took my showers and got ready at the gym and did my laundry elsewhere too. I was grateful for a place to stay rent-free but it felt sad and lonely. I was all alone and just stayed in survival mode. Sometimes, I would wake up in the middle of the night with the glowing red exit signs reminding me yet again how alone I was. The loneliness hurt so much that at times I would put on my karate uniform and go for a run to release my pain.

The Tulane Karate Club (TKC) defines *karate* as a combination of two *kanji* (Chinese characters): *kara*, meaning empty, and *te*, meaning hand; thus, karate means "empty hand." Adding the suffix "-dō" (pronounced "daw"), meaning "the way/path," karate-dō, implies karate as a total way of life that goes well beyond the self-defense applications. In traditional karate-dō, one is supposed to compete and strive to excel against him/herself." Karate was gifted to me when I didn't know how to defend myself. It saved me and gave me important life skills. I became fit and fast, confident with a healthy self-esteem. Karate had moved from just a self defense tool to becoming my second *home*. My uniform and my belt were my companion and safe place and went with me everywhere. I loved seeing them around me! It was where I felt accepted, encouraged, empowered. I could hide and be myself.

 What is your second *home*? I sacrificed a lot of time during the early years of my sport because I loved it. To this day it is still home to me. Do you have something you love that provides this type of support in your life? If so, never let it go, and keep practicing. If you left it behind, pick it back up. You need each other. The sacrifice of time to practice and learn is worth it for the sake of your soul. It will bring you through those tough patches that may be lying just ahead. Will you re-commit to your second home?

_____

_____

_____

_____

———

As I ended my second year in America, my growing belief and trust in God along with my continued practice of karate kept me going. I could work off-campus by this point so I applied to be a school bus driver! I was always fascinated by the big yellow buses I saw in the movies when I was little and dreamed of one day riding in one! The bus company let me keep the bus parked at the church. Driving through so many neighborhoods allowed me to learn a lot about the American home culture.

No matter the neighborhood, I would always see husbands in their robes, holding a coffee cup and picking up a newspaper from their front lawn which made me start dreaming of that being me one day.

The mothers would walk their children to the bus stop and always wave goodbye as we left. I loved it all and started dreaming of my own future life.

After this, I worked a series of jobs that would work around my school schedule. I worked at everything including restaurants and retail stores. I tried to learn, make more income and experiment with new environments. With each new job, I moved towards something better and higher paying. For example, I moved from JC Penney to Dillards to Nordstrom, as each one paid higher than the previous. Along the way, I was introduced to direct selling companies including the health company, USANA, which is where I started attending conferences with motivational speakers. I had already heard about Tony Robbins from a TV commercial I had seen in a friend's basement, but I hadn't heard about motivational coaching or personal leadership seminars. I was fascinated by the clothes, cars, houses and trips they showed us in their presentations, but relished their encouragement and inspiring stories the most. I was so hungry for growth, full of hope and belief that this path with direct selling companies would turn me quickly into a self-made millionaire, learning later that there is no such thing as self-made, we need each other! I desperately wanted to catch up financially, especially since I was getting older.

But there was one big opponent in my way: immigration. Immigration was my kryptonite. It kept cutting my legs back whenever I was about to fly off with an opportunity. *Lawraq. Lawraq. Lawraq.* Papers. Papers. Papers. Growing up in Tunisia we always heard the stories of those that left home to study or work abroad and if they came back without *lawraq* they were shamed by the community. If you leave your country for a significant amount of time, you have no other choice but to succeed.

To succeed abroad means you got married, had a family and made enough money to build a house back home. You were also expected to help any family member in need. No one considers going back home until they're able to prove this. Sure, your mother will accept you back regardless, however, there are no guarantees that your father will and you will definitely be shunned by everyone else. Growing up in such a culture as this, I personally knew some of the men that were unable to prove themselves and they were labeled as failures. Their stories always stuck with me.

I didn't plan on a long journey in America. I was just taking a step towards my "somewhere" when I left. But that step had now turned into four years. I was supposed to have made something of myself.

I had graduated with an Associate's Degree and although I was extremely proud of my accomplishments, especially passing College Algebra which I had to take twice, I didn't have the courage to go back yet. I didn't think I could endure the scrutiny and shame.

For four years I lived under the rule of King Immigration. I had to abide by the rules for fear of deportation, which then added to the fear of the shame I'd face once back home. I paid endless fees to stay in compliance, all the while continuing to study in a foreign language, make good grades, and work hard. I wanted to get ahead but with a twenty hour work limit, it was impossible to cover everything.

So I found myself again at a difficult crossroads. I had enrolled at the University of Kansas (KU) in Lawrence with a double major in Communications and International Studies. The fees for international students there were too high and although my student visa had "started over" at the new school, I was back to being limited to on-campus work of twenty hours a week.

To one degree or another, there are times in our lives when we face tremendous struggles that feel constrictive and make it hard to breathe. This is where I was with immigration, I was struggling to breathe. Others have similar feelings, and luckily most have nothing to do with immigration law. Regardless, their struggles are real, and in many ways may feel just the same.

One such person was someone I had met a year earlier while working at the campus gym. She had returned to school to finish an Associate's Degree and we became good friends. As our friendship grew, we shared our challenges, and while I could not make my immigration woes disappear, I might be able to help her. There were a number of heartbreaking hurdles she was facing. If I am being honest, helping her made me feel better in the face of my own challenges. It made me forget, at least for a time. I wanted to be what most of us desire to be, a hero. A knight in shining armor, or more specifically, Wyatt Earp, or John Wayne. I have always loved American westerns. Relationships that begin as a result of shared pain are often doomed, and this was but one example. Ultimately, we found ourselves talking about marriage; she wanted a family and children, and even though my gut told me it was the wrong decision, we continued down the path. The first rule, when you find yourself in a hole, is "stop digging." I ignored the rule. I was at a crossroads and the decision to marry sounded right, although the voices that I was listening to were biased. They were the voices of fear. The voice of my loneliness. The voices from my village telling me that I failed, that I had thrown in the towel. The voices that were telling me that I would never amount to anything more than a struggling immigrant who didn't belong anywhere, let alone in America. I felt like Atlas, I just wanted the weight to lighten, and with that, we got married. I knew, in my gut, that the decision was wrong, not just for me, but for her too. Ultimately, I went from the frying pan into the fire. My life was now split, trying to understand a bizarre new home life with a person with her own struggles, all while keeping the American dream of one day starting a business of my own. Despite good intentions, the relationship was emotionally destructive, and as it began, it would likewise end. All is not lost, however, because knowledge can be extracted from every situation, and this one taught me many things, such as continuing to listen to one's intuition even through extreme pain.

 Harvard Business Law says: Despite popular belief, there's a deep neurological basis for intuition. Scientists call the stomach the "second brain" for a reason. There's a vast neural network of 100 million neurons lining your entire digestive tract. That's more neurons than are found in the spinal cord, which points to the gut's incredible processing abilities.

When you approach a decision intuitively, your brain works in tandem with your gut to quickly assess all your memories, past learnings, personal needs, and preferences and then makes the wisest decision given the context. In this way, intuition is a form of emotional and experiential data that leaders need to value.

Your intuition, that gut feeling, is like the ship's rudder. It plays a very important part in the direction of your life. When it malfunctions, you end up with serious steering issues. You're going to pay a price. I now understood how it felt to be truly alone navigating life and its challenges. I wasn't successful. I don't think anyone can be alone. We don't have the capacity for it. If you currently find yourself leaning towards a decision that is contrary to the tugging of your gut, hold on just a bit longer. Don't make that decision quite yet. Get good counsel. Get to the bottom of your true motive and fear. Why are you tempted to make that decision? Don't make justification or talk yourself into thinking it'll get better after you make it. It won't get better. You're seeking the quick fix, the immediate relief to your pain. Hold on and get help. Process and come up with a solution together.

There is no wrong time to make the right decision. So if you have already chosen the opposite of your gut, then get help, recalibrate together, readjust, live the best you can through it. Learn how to lose well in order to eventually still win.

Remember, choose to conquer that fear, don't give up in seeking for true help and trust your gut! My friend, John C. Maxwell, whom I had the privilege to meet by this point, said "Everything worthwhile is uphill." Keep climbing!

CHAPTER 9
YOU CAN GET PAID FOR THAT?

 You don't have to be great to get started, but you have to get started to be great. —Les Brown

By my second semester at the University of Kansas, the fees and expenses were more than I could financially manage. I had borrowed student loans, which my dear friend Brian had co-signed for, and I was still unable to meet the financial demand. Withdrawing from school was the best decision. The choice was difficult, but nonetheless, I went back to the drawing board to work on getting ahead of the curve.

I found work for multiple companies, ranging from Sprint, Citibank, UPS, FedEx and overnight security. I wasn't afraid of the hard work, but most offered limited income options only ranging as high as 17 USD per hour and none of them spoke to my desire for growth. I wanted the American dream for the sake of my own validation and belonging. I was hungry to prove I could keep up with all those motivational speakers showing off their big homes and fancy cars.

A Polish friend named Edita called me one day to say hello. During our conversation, she told me she had been hired as an interpreter. I didn't understand. "They pay you for that?" I asked. She said she was making 35 USD per hour, getting two hours minimum per job and mileage reimbursed. I could not believe it! I asked her for the contact information and called right away to get an interview. I was trained and was hired for my first job two days later! It was finally the breakthrough I had been seeking. The floodgates were opened, the jobs were pouring in for my two language pairings. Another step toward my "somewhere!"

Within two months, I was working nonstop. I was unleashed from my work limitations by then and I felt alive and with more drive than I had ever experienced before. I was back on the road going from place to place, sometimes up to five different job locations in a single day. I was absolutely every-where; courts, attorney's offices, hospitals, clinics, home visits, schools, restaurants, and even military bases. I accepted every job offer, hating to miss any of them. If I could have worked 24/7, I absolutely would have. I loved everything about the industry! The speed of it, the variety, the clients, the money, all of it. It was exhilarating and exhausting, in a good way, and I was happy.

I kept this speed up for two solid years. Every opportunity that came my way talking about growth, I took as well. I wasn't just hungry, I was starving for it. I inhaled it all and tried to apply the principles I was learning immediately to my new life as an interpreter. But, I was too busy and going a little too fast to absorb all the knowledge that I was trying so earnestly to learn.

In January of 2007, while I was attending a personal growth seminar in San Francisco, I was sitting in a coffee shop reflecting on the previous day's activities. It seemed like my language and cultural barriers always got in the way. I wanted to be truly understood and to truly understand others. Instantly a feeling washed over me and I knew in my gut that I needed to start a language company to help solve this dilemma —I wanted to help bridge that gap of misunderstandings. I wrote the name "Bridging the Gap Interpreting" on a napkin and tucked it away in my notebook.

I got back to Kansas City and continued the pace and rhythm I had been on for the next several months. By June of that year, I knew I couldn't keep going at that speed. I wanted to duplicate myself. I knew that I needed to hire others to represent me. With the help of my British friend Mike from his basement computer, I officially registered Bridging the Gap Interpreting

(BTGI) as an LLC in the state of Kansas on June 27, 2007. I didn't know how to run a business. But I knew sales, and also if others could do it, so could I. I didn't need a "four-year plan." I just needed to take the first step. As Les Brown says, "just get started." I was back to my roots.

Mike helped me create business cards, brochures, and a webpage. Bart and Kristy, friends who hosted me for two weeks in their home while I was transitioning my housing, wanted to hear all about my company and ended up helping me with round two of these marketing tools. I stopped accepting jobs from other companies so I could focus on growing my own, but I did go back to working security overnight so I could support myself in the meantime. I didn't let any opportunity to network pass without telling them about my company and discovering if they needed my services. Through word of mouth, I was getting a steady flow of requests!

Passion and excitement really opened doors. I presented my company with such conviction that no one would turn me away. One time, I received a request for a Spanish interpreter, and instead of saying no, I accepted and went out and found a Spanish interpreter to hire for the job! From that point forward, I knew I wanted to offer language services in all languages.

A few months into my new routine, I received a call to cover a last-minute overnight security shift for someone, and wanting to help, I accepted. I was wearing my black khaki suit and I had the security company shirt and my badge with me. To make the shift on time, I decided my uniform was close enough, as the only thing my pants did not have were a simple yellow stripe down the outside seam!

At about mid-shift, my manager stopped by to conduct a location check. He looked at my pants and asked, "why are you out of uniform?" I tried to explain my thinking and my desire to be on time to cover my co-worker's shift, but despite my explanation, he went beyond, chastising me for not being in full uniform. He was angry and yelling at me. I realized then, I needed to resign. The security job provided a steady income and I was afraid to rely solely on my company supporting me, but in that moment, I gained courage. I had been reading *The Compassionate Samurai* by Brian Klemmer which gave me the extra support and confirmation I needed to move on. I turned in my keys and walked away. The following morning, I was full of fire and determination to make *my* business successful!

The power of closed doors, willingly or unwillingly, are important to discuss when it comes to personal growth. I was reduced to nothing at a job that I only had because of fear of financial security. Sun Tzu in *The Art of War* states, "When your army has crossed the border, you should burn your boats and bridges, in order to make it clear to everybody that you have no hankering after home." The action of turning in my keys was me burning my *ship* and choosing to embrace the challenge ahead of me with no other option but to win!

For the next two years, I lived and breathed my company. My first bookkeeper was a Filipino woman named Pam, that I had struck up a conversation with at Costco, one of my favorite retailers and most dependable networking secrets! My first inclination was that she might be interested in learning about working as an interpreter. Through our conversation, I discovered she was a CPA. She couldn't help with interpreting but could help with my daily invoicing and became my very first bookkeeper! Stefanie, Jean, and her daughter Rebekah followed in Pam's footsteps bookkeeping for BTGI in different seasons. Each of them became a lifeline for whom I am forever grateful.

My other lifeline, karate, was still by my side too. I decided to open a karate school so I could share my skills with others. I called it "Karate For Life" and offered classes at different churches, community centers, and schools.

It was a challenge carrying equipment and uniforms in the back of my SUV, yet, it was rewarding teaching kids and parents my skill set. I met a set of parents that couldn't afford tuition so I asked if they'd like to volunteer to run the administration side of things. They gladly did. Later, when I found myself needing another scheduler for BTGI, I asked if they'd like the job. They worked with me for about a year and then I started getting a bad gut feeling about them. Things weren't adding up. Our conversations weren't solving the problems, and I knew I needed to dismiss them. I notified them and set up a time to meet to get the company's computer and phone back two days later. During those two days, I later found out they had downloaded my list of clients and interpreters that I had worked so hard to compile and chose to continue doing *my* business under a new company name.

This couple had pitched their services to all of my clients at a cheaper rate so they would be awarded the jobs and were reaching out to my list of interpreters that I had trained. They were billing the clients, but not paying the interpreters, so it became a disaster for me. The interpreters were accustomed to this couple working in my company, so they thought they were still working for me when they got offers from them and chose to accept the jobs. I was devastated! I reached out to every client and interpreter I knew who had been affected. Unfortunately, some clients chose to stay with them because of the cheaper rate and some interpreters chose to not believe it had not been my company that had sent them. I won as many back as I could, but my reputation had taken a major blow. I experienced my first betrayal within a company setting.

Feeling like I was back at ground zero, I chose to go full speed ahead to rebuild my company. I hired another scheduler and kept pressing on gaining traction again with new clients and interpreters. I spoke to everyone, everywhere! No matter where I was or what I was doing, it was automatic. If I heard even a hint of an accent in someone, I started a conversation with them and let them know about my company. I met people everywhere; gas stations, grocery stores, restaurants, parking lots, anywhere! And if they were interested but had never interpreted before, I offered them training.

At some point in 2009, I remember an assignment that made a tremendous impact on me. I had been called in by the police to be the interpreter for a house call. Arriving at the apartment in a very difficult neighborhood, I discovered the family, a couple and two children, were from Togo who had arrived in America via the Visa Lottery about two years before. They had borrowed money to travel to America and couldn't wait to begin living out the "American Dream." They were rich in their home country, but in America, the best job the husband could get without knowing English was a pizza delivery driver. Life had taken a toll on him and his family. He thought he'd be able to pay back the borrowed money very quickly. However, things turned out a lot differently than expected. He had become angry and violent, and now, they found themselves with their children about to be taken away. At that moment, I felt a transition from being an interpreter to becoming a life coach. Something changed in my soul. America had beaten them up (I understood!), but they were making their pit deeper and deeper by turning to violence. It killed me inside to know their children might be taken away. I wanted to encourage them. But…I was just the interpreter, plus, I was still struggling too. So I filed this moment away for the time being, although more and more stories like this one kept coming across my interpreting path.

The next two years were *une saison que j'ai perdu mes pédals*. It was a blur. A mixture of good and bad. My personal life was getting worse and my capacity to keep running the business was strained. Despite this, I had wonderful opportunities as an interpreter, including being trained to be an Arabic language tester. My training was completed in New York City, with another language teaching organization, and it was not only a great opportunity but a tremendous life event too. The activities of life were certainly enough to keep me busy, but the nagging question was, "what was I busy doing?" I was losing my pedals internally. It had been over ten years since I had seen my family, and that was deeply painful, and emotional, and it was killing me from the inside. I desperately needed to recenter; I needed to go *home*. I didn't have much money, but after receiving my first Green Card, I started saving as much as I could until I gathered enough money to travel. My American friend, Mike, donated his miles for my round trip ticket and I prepared to go see my family, to see *Ommi*.

On September 30, 2010 I boarded a plane back to Tunisia. It should have been one of the happiest days of my life, but instead I was dreading the cultural battle. I had missed the two-year mark, the five-year mark, and even the eight-year mark of returning home in glory. All seemingly invisible marks, but they are very real within my culture. By the tenth year of being away without going back, the cultural expectation is that you are now a multimillionaire, and to prove it, you better be arriving with suitcases bursting at the seams full of money. An intense amount of emotional pressure is placed on you, both from being away so long and from the feeling of abandoning your family and community. So here I am, on a plane back home, with a suitcase filled with just my few clothes, books, and my beloved karate uniform. I had made a conscious decision to face my fear because I didn't want these expectations and cultural control to keep me away any longer. I missed my family, and I desperately needed to go *home*.

On my layover in France, I met with an old roommate while I lived in Tunis and dear friend, Mounir. He provided me with a much needed sounding board to talk and process the things I was about to encounter and experience when I arrived. He asked me if I had gifts to present when I reached Tunis, and when I told him that I did not, he promptly said, "that will not do." He then went to the chocolatier and purchased gift boxes of chocolates for me, so that I would not arrive empty-handed. I reflect on this gesture of kindness to this day and I am grateful for his sensitivity, and understanding.

My entire family greeted me like a movie star at the airport. It was overwhelming and wonderful to see so many familiar faces. Some were taller, some had a few more kids, while others had more gray hairs and wrinkles. They were all beautiful to me. I felt instantly loved and accepted. Arriving home, my sister Samira was the first to see me. She literally fainted! I picked her back up, and she didn't want to let me go. Then I saw *Ommi*, and my heart was immediately comforted. She wouldn't let me go either, hugging me so tightly around my neck. *Ashrra ssniin! Ashrra ssniin!* "Ten years," she kept saying, over and over, "ten years!" Weeping, *Ommi* cried, "My son is home, my son is home, I can finally touch your face again." My culture is transfixed with food, and my arrival was not any different. They cooked, and we stayed up well into the late hours of the night talking. From that point forward, my month back home felt like the first month I spent in America in 1999. It was a complete whirlwind.

In America I was going from home to home and felt the pressure of all their questions about who I was, where I came from and what it was like in Africa. Now, my family were all coming to me, and meeting me with silent stares. After the initial hugs and kisses when someone would arrive, they'd sit waiting for me to bring out gifts. They killed you with silence if you didn't live up to the expectation. They wanted what America meant to them: money and gifts. I was constantly unnerved and remained with my guard up every single day, battling between the pressure I was under and just wanting to enjoy being home. The expectations weren't ever verbal but they were present and made the air very thick. I wanted to reconnect and have a peaceful time, but the culture was bombarding me. I never knew who was going to arrive that day and what they were hoping to receive. My mother and sister were pressured to prepare meals for everyone too. Even my sister had gone out to buy more chocolates to give on my behalf. It was a very bitter-sweet time and, before long, the stress became such a constant drain that unfortunately, I just wanted the trip to end. I was not the hero they expected. My trip came to a close after a month. I kissed *Ommi* goodbye through streams of tears and returned to Kansas City with an awful gut feeling, and another nagging question, "where do I belong now?"

How could I possibly unpack and process all of the experiences and feelings that I had? Home was where I would receive support, encouragement, and acceptance. Now, home felt like I was trying to net a butterfly's shadow. I would swing my net, only to have it flutter away once more. My *home* had changed a lot in my absence. It seemed like I didn't belong to the world I was leaving and as I flew back to Kansas, I wasn't sure I fit into the world I was flying towards either. I was no longer Tunisian enough nor had I become American enough yet, so who was I? I do not remember if I knew the definition of enigma at the time, but as I sat in my return coach class seat, I am certain I felt like one. It was a strange feeling indeed.

I became a U.S. citizen on July 29, 2011. It was a day I'll never forget. The endless filing of applications and interviews and living in fear of doing anything out of compliance or the heavy weight of all the limitations was finally lifted. My *lawraq* were permanent. Over two hundred people came out to the ceremony to support me (that's the true beauty of the power of connectivity!) so the officials had to open an overflow room for them. Afterwards, we had a celebratory meal. It was an incredibly emotional experience for which I am forever grateful.

All of the pain and sacrifice led to this very moment! And then, when it's all over and everyone goes home, you start to ask yourself if it was worth it? My culture said, get *lawraq*, get married, have a house, and come back and we'll all call you successful! I was miserable. I did not ascribe to my culture's definition of success; my belief is that success is connected to pursuing your purpose and meaning. I have been in constant motion to find my path since I was a little boy in my hometown. All of my tours and detours placed me in North America and I was now the recipient of the coveted Citizenship award - I had reached the peak of my summit! Or had I? There were plenty of things I learned and acquired through this journey, but how could I piece it all together into finding my true purpose and meaning? "Welcome to the United States of America. Now you have the legal right to vote and to change or modify your name if you choose to" said the Immigration Officer after being approved for citizenship. I was taken aback at first but then immediately said, "yes, my name will be Nabil Cherif." Cherif is my *Babba's* first name who I always wanted to carry closer to me so this was my chance. Our family surname is Jemai, which I love and honor, I just wanted to also be known by being *his* son in particular from our Jemai tribe. I was symbolically using this as my first step into finding *my* true identity, purpose and meaning. I honor *Ommi* by living out the meaning of my first name Nabil, and I'm taking *Babba* along with me in my journey through my last name Cherif. Our first and last names are outward representations of who we are internally.

 What does your name mean to you? Maybe the definition of your name itself has a special meaning you'd like to live up to, or maybe you're defining the meaning of your name as you journey along, or maybe it needs to be changed to better represent the legacy you'd like others to inherit. The point is, your name should be unique to you and you should be proud and smile every time you hear someone call it out, even if it's mispronounced! You are seen and heard by your name, it's who *you* are, hold onto it! And as *Ommi* always told me, I too hope you're living up to the meaning of your name! "Names are the sweetest and most important sound in any language." —Dale Carnegie

---

My business was continuing to grow, and I desperately needed to find office support again. I hired a husband and wife team who came highly recommended to work as schedulers, along with managing the bookkeeping. However, a year later, I got a nagging feeling in my gut again. Business had slowed down and we weren't seeing eye-to-eye on how to run the company.

My personal life was at its lowest point, and on May 3, 2012, I filed for personal bankruptcy. I was at a loss, and I needed inspiration, and answers, so I hit the road living out of a 1999 Ford Econoline conversion van and trailer that I sold almost everything to acquire. I always loved to drive, and the open road comforted me and gave me time to think. I interpreted over the phone to support myself while I figured out how to keep BTGI going.

I returned after three months, nothing had really changed. I hit the road again, this time in a 2006 Toyota Avalon that I found for sale in Chicago. I took the overnight mega bus so that I could arrive at the dealership in the early morning hours to convince them to sell me the car. I had terrible credit, but at my core I am a communicator and that coupled with the grace of God I convinced them to sell me the car. The 11.5% interest rate for a used car felt usury, but I did not have a choice, I needed a car. I had sold my conversion van to pay bills and I was intent on meeting a family in Idaho that I had met several months prior. The power of connections can be amazing, and in this case, I had met the family during a karate event. Their plan was to travel the U.S. in their RV and offer karate seminars, essentially creating a mobile karate studio and I liked the idea. I also liked their RV idea and kept an eye out for an opportunity to buy one for myself.

On my way to Idaho I passed by an RV sales lot in Spokane, Washington with motorhomes festooned with multicolored vinyl flags flapping in the breeze. One caught my eye and I stopped to look. My credit rating had not improved since I started my trip, but I did have 6,000 USD cash, and the 1994 Winnebago Itasca was reduced from 15,600 USD to 7,500 USD. I offered the 6,000 USD that I had but was refused, so I countered with 6,200 USD, and the deal was done! I was in my first home, I was free! I set up my office to continue operating as a phone interpreter and started working from home, well before the concept was mainstream! I was back on the road with my Avalon in tow to meet up with the family in Idaho.

After a few days in Idaho, the plan was to travel, train, and teach karate. The experience was great, but we were constantly separated. It felt like I was chasing them, or they were chasing me. I was growing tired of this lifestyle and decided it was best to part ways and I hit the road with my Garmin recalculated to my "somewhere."

I checked on my business every day, calling my office to speak with staff. During one of my calls my office told me they had found an interpreter to hire for a court job. After reading her resume, I hired her immediately. Days later I spoke to her on the phone. As I continued to travel south on the Pacific Coast Highway, I thought about my conversation with her while quickly switching gears as I headed toward San Diego, where I had previously spent time and loved. There was something about San Diego that reminded me of home. As I drove through northern California, I passed through the mountainous Sierras whose elevation and steep downhill grades made driving my motorhome a challenge, more so while towing my Avalon! The trip was not easy, and on more than a few occasions, I was certain I was going to be involved in a Michael Bay directed Hollywood movie-style accident. My overheating motorhome chugged up one side of the inclines and schussed down the other. There were times that I was standing on the gas pedal while blasting the heater to counter the engine heat. This trick was one that I learned from several truck drivers I met on my way. I was not an over-the-road trucker, but I did enjoy being in a fraternity of big rigs. As I made my way south, I roamed, circled, and backtracked. First Sacramento, then Los Angeles, back to San Jose, San Francisco, and finally, my destination of San Diego.

During my daily calls to the office, I was informed how well the new interpreter was doing with our court sessions. Legal sessions are challenging, not only due to the formalities, but with the judges, attorneys, court reporters, plaintiffs, defendants, and galleries, it can seem like a three-ring circus. To find an interpreter that could not only manage the language aspect, but do so under the proverbial Big Top was a coup, so I was encouraged to hear this report. I called her a second time to thank her. Whether or not that second phone call had anything to do with an audible voice I began to hear as I continued to set up residence in San Diego is perhaps better left to others, but regardless, the voice was telling me to go back to Kansas City. I ignored it at first because it was the last thing I wanted to do. I was now divorced and didn't have the capacity to return to Kansas City. I was done with my past, and Kansas City was in my past. Try as I might though, I began to feel like my past was not done with me, and my gut was telling me that I needed to pull stakes and head back east to Kansas. So I did, and the day after I arrived, I met this mysterious new interpreter, Emily.

Emily, just born in Keflavik, Iceland!

CHAPTER 10
WHO IS THIS GUY?

CONTRIBUTED BY EMILY CHERIF

 *Fear has two meanings: 'Forget Everything And Run'
or 'Face Everything And Rise.' The choice is yours. —
Zig Ziglar*

Our story has reached an inflection point and from here
forward, the reader will be invited to be an insider, and
collaborator. The reader is offered a rare look into a relationship
that is deeply personal, and is driven by the challenges of a
business, marriage, personal independence, and love. This is
the part that asks the reader to challenge one's priorities by
asking what is the most important thing that I must do at any
given moment? And, how can I balance these priorities, which
may be conflicting, to the best of one's ability?

" Hi! I'm Emily. I was born in Iceland to a Costa Rican mother and a North American father who had joined the Air Force. My father's first station was Keflavik Air Base where my brother and I were born. My mom raised us, speaking only Spanish. The only time we spoke English at home was when speaking to my dad. I went to 4th grade at a school in Lancaster, CA.

My dad was stationed at Edwards AFB, about 45 min away from where we lived. My school had very few Hispanic students, and one day the principal came into our classroom asking if anyone knew Spanish in order to interpret for a family in his office. I immediately shot up my hand and almost fell out of my chair with excitement. I was a very shy girl, but, at that moment, I felt confident and courageous! I loved speaking Spanish, and for the first time I was using it to help complete strangers.

Ten years later, I completed my first year at Longview Community College in Kansas City, MO. My advisor recommended that I choose an International Business major, but I hated it. I felt lost and sat at my kitchen table completely distraught. I believe in the power of prayer, and as I was journaling, praying, and reading the Bible, God led me to some passages specifically talking about the gift of interpreting. Through those passages, I gained clarity, and at that moment, I knew my career. I was going to be an interpreter!

" The very next day I switched my major to Spanish and French since there wasn't an actual interpreting degree back then. As soon as I graduated from college, I was off to conquer the world! Another ten years passed, and I found myself at another crossroads. Although I occasionally interpreted, it was not what my full-time job required. I felt alone and unfulfilled. I remember reading the book *9 Things A Leader Must Do* by Dr. Henry Cloud at lunch one day. I didn't even get through Chapter 1 before completely melting down. Cloud talked about digging deep to discover your gifts and talents. He pointed out that it's up to YOU to develop them! I had just been relying on my team for interpreting opportunities. I knew I was a good interpreter, but I wasn't taking it into my own hands to develop. The book made me realize it was up to ME!

" I knew at that moment, I needed to resign and discover my path as a freelance interpreter. I immediately joined the local memberships, got Missouri state court certified and looked into schools where I could get a Master's degree in Interpreting. I felt alive again!

" I started freelancing with Bridging the Gap Interpreting, LLC during this time period in early 2013.
The owner, Nabil Cherif, hired me right away to
interpret and lead the interpreter training. During
one of these training sessions, I met the owner in
person. He burst into the coffee shop where I was
meeting an interpreter, whom I was training. He
appeared to visit each table in the coffee shop,
greeting everyone. From my vantage, he seemed to
talk to everyone in the room. I had never seen
anyone do this before. "Who is this guy?!"

" Four months later, we got married on March 13,
2014! What a plot twist! We did not take a honeymoon, at first anyway, which is certainly not an
unusual situation, many couples do not take a
honeymoon. Ours was delayed due to the fact that
BTGI was clearly being mismanaged and something needed to be done. The more layers of the
onion that we peeled, the depth of mishandling

bordered on willful negligence, and Nabil knew he had to take back control. After months of long days, and long nights cleaning up the books, processing past due invoices and timesheets, often taking us into the wee hours of the morning, the company was out of the woods and ready to continue. In addition to now running the business, both of us continued to interpret too. Nabil would take the French and Arabic assignments, and I would do the Spanish ones. If he was on a job, I would be in the car working the business until he finished. He'd then drive me to my job. Every day was different and full of adventure, but we loved what we were doing!

From the moment I met Emily, I felt like I could breathe again, and I knew I would marry her. All of my years searching for home, and I found it; not in a place, or a house, but rather in a person. She was my person, and she was my *home*. Emily filled the emptiness inside of me. Our marriage renewed me and led me to a brand new season of life. Despite all of my mistakes, I was offered hope. My pillars of health started functioning again and my inner strength and stability returned. I was not sure I deserved such grace, but miraculously, when I was absolutely at the end of myself, God picked me up and helped me begin again. Our first two years were a whirlwind with the company. My health returned, and I was reinspired to make my business flourish! After rebranding, I hit the road promoting the business everywhere, unfortunately still with my knack for speeding tickets!

Things were very different this time because Emily was by my side. We were the duo I never thought could exist. The next two years, we ran the company remotely from Chicago, even though everyone thought we were crazy to move to such a cold city, which they proved to be right after I was hospitalized with pneumonia!

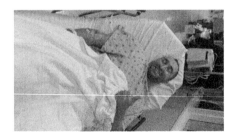

Emily got her license as an Illinois state court interpreter and led the company. I went back to school full-time. This time, my studies were focused inwardly, versus outward attainment of status. I realize that each of us comes to enlightenment at our own speed, but for me, I was willing to look at all aspects of my life. My studies approached philosophical topics that are impossible to answer in a single sentence. Furthermore, I wasn't seeking to confirm that what I believed was right, or wrong, but rather, what moved me and directed me?

All of the good that has occurred to me has been the result of listening to that distinct, clear voice, directing me towards something greater than myself. I attribute this voice to God, but you the reader may attribute it to something else. The attribution is not necessary to dwell upon, the results speak for themselves. When I listen, the outcome is one that offers me the opportunity for a richer, fuller and more purposeful life.

One of my professors, seventy-five-year-old Dr. Marty was instrumental in guiding me through these questions as he quickly became a father figure. He was "for me" from my first class with him, always listening to any question I had and encouraging me, sometimes even with just a genuine smile and hug. I didn't get to conclude my studies at the Institute but the two-year relocation blessed me with another *champion* in my life and that was more than I could have asked for.

Sometimes in life, it is plenty to come out on the other side of a particular journey with just another *champion* on your side! The company was steadily growing and as our revenue increased, we were equal parts excited and exhausted. During this time I began to become aware of the spiritual, physical, and emotional scars built up in my life, and they were manifesting themselves in ways of which I wasn't proud. I was constantly engaged in a mode of survival, of winning and losing, getting ahead, and proving myself. These aspects, by themselves, are not necessarily destructive and can propel one to be a better version of themselves. However, done blindly, and without regard to others, it can be ruinous. The effects were taking a toll on my new bride, and I worried that I would lose what I treasured most.

My drive has always led my life. I will keep trying until I succeed. I don't see the obstacles–only possibilities. I will not be defeated because I didn't try. I will never pack up my bags and choose the chicken exit without giving it my best shot. Life is an equal opportunity employer; success is available for anyone willing to not let fear hold them back. This is who I am. I wasn't born to go home. The key to success in business, I believe, is this drive and desire to succeed.

One such moment stands clearly in my mind as I was on a sales trip in Wichita, KS. My final meeting had not been confirmed until almost the end of the day. The gatekeeper at the firm I was to meet with told my office manager in no uncertain terms that there was "no need to come, your bid was not chosen." When I received the news and was told that I had lost the bid and that I could just go home now, I immediately responded, "I wasn't born to go home." I drove to the building, which now closed for the day, but I knocked on the locked glass doors anyway. I kept knocking, waiting for a few beats between each successive rap on the door, and a few moments later, a figure from the inside emerged, and I was welcomed by the head of the entire department. He escorted Emily and I to their conference room and asked about our business. While he could not award us the proposal, he did call five of his colleagues at other offices to introduce BTGI. This is why you don't "just go home" at the first sign of rejection or defeat. A no is not definitive, it might mean no at the moment, but it is important to continue asking to find any other possible open doors. My gut told me to drive to this office, and it has continued to pay off in tangible and intangible ways beyond my imagination.

———————

 Is there an area in your life where you have taken the chicken exit? If you are unfamiliar with the chicken exit, I am referring to the exit that greets you just before you sit down in the car on the rollercoaster, or the one at the top of the tallest waterslide. You have made the long trek to the top, step after step, and now at the precipice, your rubber innertube draped like a giant Cheerio over your arm, you see the sloshing water and hear the peals and shrieks of others. Glancing around, instead of pushing that last final step, you see the Chicken Exit sign. Your choice made, down you walk, dejected and unhappy. I am not calling you a chicken, I am asking, what is stopping you? Why did you choose to go home, instead of making the leap? Fear? Insecurity? Procrastination? Discomfort? If you want to pierce through the sound barrier of your current situation, you have to choose courage. Chuck Yeager said, *"We didn't know if we could break the sound barrier. But it was our duty to try. That's the way I looked at it."* Capt. Charles Yeager was the first pilot to break the speed of sound on October 14, 1947. Up until that point it had been an impossible dream for fear of what may happen from a supersonic flight hitting an invisible barrier. Yeager took the chance and made history. It's your duty to find out what may happen if *you* take your life to supersonic levels and break through your sound barrier. You never know, you may make history of your own! Remember Zig Ziglar's advice, choose to face things instead of running "home" from them.

All of this is a no-brainer in our professional and business lives, but does that same hold true in marriage?

CHAPTER 11
WAIT, WHAT?

CONTRIBUTED BY EMILY CHERIF

> *Hardships often prepare ordinary people for an extraordinary destiny.* —C.S. Lewis

~

By 2018, I started my annual journal with the goal of leaving the company by July 30th. It had been four years of nonstop work and the business had taken a major toll on me mentally and emotionally and the stress was manifesting itself physically through weight gain. I desperately wanted to return to my fitness. The day-to-day problems were overwhelming. Date nights weren't about us having a nice dinner and conversation together. They always turned into networking opportunities with anyone that could be a potential partnership for the business. Even grocery shopping would turn into work. We both enjoy cooking, so grocery shopping was a fun chore for us until it turned into the job. If Nabil would hear someone talking with an accent in the store, he would go talk to them about the business. There was nothing off-limits. As we pumped gas, I'd hear him talking to the car next to us. Going for walks, if no one was around to talk to, undoubtedly the phone would ring with a company issue to be resolved or a last minute job offer for the next day. It was back to work.

I couldn't take the stress of it all, was not exercising daily anymore, chose other ways to decompress, and in turn, each year that went by gifted me with ten extra pounds. I had lost control of my daily routine and found myself completely trapped in a body I no longer recognized in the mirror.

July 30th came and went. I was still working. As soon as we got a break, something would happen requiring my full attention. As 2019 began, my resolutions stayed the same. This year, I vowed to make it happen. We moved back to Kansas City and bought a home with room for a home office and meeting space. We had a great team in place. Then a team member left. The default solution was that I would take their place, so I did! Although I had the same goal in 2020, the year-end result was the same. Another team member left. By 2021 we were down to only one employee, and the global pandemic was in full swing. We were not alone in its destructive effects, but when it is your business, it is hard not to take lost business personally. The downsizing of our team had been inevitable. The company was still going strong as the need for our services didn't disappear–just changed from in-person to mostly online. Through the government assistance for small businesses, we invested in staff and worked to rebuild with the intention of freeing me from the day-to-day operations once and for all. Unfortunately, my yearly ten-pound gift was still in effect.

At the beginning of 2022, two more members were hired including a Director of Operations/Human Resources. Could the end finally be in sight? One more hiccup hit us when we were down another teammate and I dutifully stepped back in. We rehired quickly and got them fully trained. By May, I was on a plane to Orlando headed to "the happiest place on earth" and had completely logged out of every company account! It felt like the dreamteam was finally in place and I was out!

"The resort had a beautiful pool with a waterfall where I could hang out, the water symbolically washing away the years of stress, and its noise drowning out the sound of my tears and pain. I didn't know how to process my last eight years of life. Wait, what?

What just happened? Was it really over? Eight years was a long detour from where I thought I was heading when we first got married. Right before meeting Nabil, I was moving to Geneva, Switzerland to get my master's degree in conference interpreting. But having put that dream on the back burner, did I even still want it? Back then I was in my mid-thirties and was already going to be the oldest in the program, and now it was worse, it was eight years later and I was in my forties! And then, what about just being an interpreter in general?

 How did I even process if I was still meant to be an interpreter too? Was I just burnt out and some rest would eventually cure me? Was my journey as an interpreter over? Through journaling and meditation, God reminded me that interpreting was given to me as a GIFT. It was not a career choice but a calling. I cried and cried! When we face times of deconstruction, we break ourselves down to our individual parts to be able to reinterpret them and start rebuilding again. For me, when it comes to interpreting, the purest form of that part of me IS my ten-year-old self. That's the anchor to which I seem to return, it's one of MY homes. I know now that it will always be there with me moving forward.

On October 5th I participated in a women's leadership conference as an attempt to connect with someone who would hear my inner cry for help. I was lost professionally, emotionally and physically. Would I ever be that leader I craved to be? Was there hope for healing the wounds of my last eight years? Would I ever get my body back? I had tried to help myself over the years, but that's just it, I was trying to help me. I didn't resort to asking for outside help, partly because of lack of time and bandwidth to research the right resources, but more so because I realized I had stopped caring about my wellbeing. There was no time for that, and as long as the business was getting taken care of, I convinced myself that was enough. Through tears, I talked to many of the conference speakers I felt a connection with during their speeches. As a result of asking for help, which you can't just wish for silently and expect someone to know you need help, you have to verbalize your needs, I was able to find a mentor, a licensed counselor AND a health coach. It seemed that by being vulnerable and unleashing my inner cry for help, I had been heard and no one turned me down!

My 2023 goals no longer needed to include taking a back seat to our beloved company, just my inner and outer fitness now. Regaining myself. I'm committed to taking the time necessary to fully heal, be restored and become an even better version of myself. I don't regret the last eight years, but I eventually would if I continued on the path I was on. I believe, in my heart, that these years were meant to be preparation for what is to come.

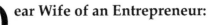

Dear Wife of an Entrepreneur:

Please don't feel like entrepreneurship is your destiny just because you married into it. I know it's trendy and glorious to label yourself as a "couplepreneur." There are many who do it successfully, but is that really who YOU are? If it is, perfect! Conquer the world of business together as a team. Hit the road, do all of the events and meetings, make lots of money, but just don't hoard it, give back for the greater good. There's a unique purpose for "couplepreneurship," I believe in it! There's power in being a team! It's just not for me. And if it isn't for you either, stop. Get out. Or at least get out for a while to reassess and make sure of what you truly desire. It may take some time to get out because we DO want to help. If there's a need, we'll naturally and instinctively jump in. But there is ALWAYS going to be a need in the entrepreneurial world, and without realizing it because it's so fast-paced, you too will have put your personal wellbeing on the back burner. Don't give up on yourself. If you know you need to stop, keep writing your goals and stating them to your entrepreneur spouse so you can plan your exit together. Then keep striving to accomplish them until you finally do! It took me five years, maybe it will take you a lot less but I don't believe it should take you a lot more. You have your own set of gifts and calling that you need to develop and share with the world. Be intentional to believe in them, fight for them and go out and conquer your piece of the world with it. Then, you and your spouse can come together for dinner each night rejoicing and sharing each other's accomplishments - NOT the problems. Save that for the team you hired. Bring your best self to the table and refresh each other's soul. If you have a family and dinner doesn't lend itself to this kind of talk, then make it non-negotiable to spend time together at some point throughout the day. Spend time talking, listening and building each other up for the next day, whether it is every day life or conquering the world!

—Emily Cherif

Winter in Ain Draham!

CHAPTER 12
SLOWING DOWN TO SPEED UP?

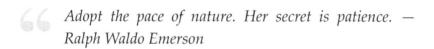

Adopt the pace of nature. Her secret is patience. — *Ralph Waldo Emerson*

I have always lived in the mid-latitude region of the world, so I've been privileged to experience four climatic seasons each year. Winter is a time when nature rests and stores up energy in order for new growth in the spring. Growing up in Tunisia, winter would bring a lot of snowstorms in my village. Heavy snow would blanket the entire area, and people would drive from all parts of the country to come see our snow. Sometimes the snow made opening the front door of our home impossible, so winter was definitely a season for which we had to prepare, including making enough couscous to last us through the harsh season; *Ommi* would sometimes prepare up to 150 kilos before winter!

We would have it with milk and raisins for breakfast and with lamb meat, if we had any, and vegetables for lunch and dinner, along with plenty of *harissa* of course! I loved this of year and the peace I felt just watching the snowfall from the window or playing with it outside even though I didn't have any gloves. *Ommi* seemed to sense when it was going to be a big snowfall too as it would get extremely quiet outside right before the storm. Stuck inside, I loved playing cards with my family or just listening to *Ommi* tell stories by the fire as she made delicious *tabouna* or *mlewi* on the flat chimney stone. To this day, I'm not sure if the stories were true or made up!

Getting ready for winter was a must, being unprepared was not an option. Once winter arrived, we were able to enjoy it from the comfort of our home. Similarly, the year 2022 became a time for me and BTGI to embrace the winter season. BTGI turned fifteen years old, and it had gone through just about as much as I had until that point! Staff came and went for both good and bad reasons. The company has had wins and losses, been rebranded, been lied to and had its information stolen. But, as Maxwell says, "Sometimes you win, sometimes you learn." On the other side, it has also served the greater Kansas City community and beyond with the gift of language. Its ability to "bridge the gap" between communication barriers has been relentless. We should have been forced to stop operating many times, but yet we pressed forward, coming back stronger and stronger each time. There's a bigger reason than my understanding of why it has stayed alive through all of the challenges, plus a worldwide pandemic. I want to honor its continued existence, growth and maturity. So then, how did we both "winter" well in order to be ready for growth in the "spring"?

Author Chris McAlister from *The Stuck Book* says that winter should be a time for the following (my additions in bullets):

"Winter: Clarity > Intensity"

• As a company, we chose to take a step back from the intensity of sales and marketing. We worked to clarify our core values and how they factor into the work we do everyday. As a result, we chose to walk away from any client or associate who didn't line up with what we stand for. These core values have been the theme of our journey: Drive, Enrichment, Fairness and Empathy. We choose to never give up, learn as much as we can along the way, pass it on, treat all equally, do our best to listen and relate to you and each other sincerely from the heart.

• My wife always says that I am the most intense person she has ever met. I know she's right. I have been in survivor mode for as long as I can remember. I need to learn how to scale back such an intense approach to life so I can clarify my future vision and goals. I need to not feel like I'm on the defensive side all of the time. I need to take time to plan out my next move instead of just reacting to everything that comes my way. It's not easy to change this habit, but, with accountability and the right coach, I know I can learn to spend more time on the offensive.

• How can you make clarity be greater than your intensity for a season?

_____

_____

_____

"Grieve what was lost or stolen."

• BTGI has much to grieve over lost sales and stolen information. We acknowledged our past pain and came up with tools to help us through future grieving of any hits the company may receive.

• I have much to grieve. My choice to come to America left me with the loss of my family and community. I lost my culture and language along with a familiar and comfortable environment. I lost seeing my nieces and nephews grow up (24 of them!) and coffee times and walks in the woods with my brothers. I lost my best friend Moncef a few months after moving to America from a heart attack. My dear brother Mahmood passed away and my dear friend Khaled. My Jaddi and Jidda (grandparents) also passed away shortly after my move to America. I lost my freedom to come and go. To grieve these years and the losses was no small task. Avoidance has not made the feelings go away, and it was my intention through this "Winter season" to expose my pain and embrace the healing process.

• What loss do you need to still grieve?

_____

_____

_____

_____

"Do you feel like you've reached the bottom or end of your motivation?"

• The hardest part of running a company seems to be employing staff that are truly called, connected and passionate about the nature of the business. As soon as it seems you have built the dreamteam, something happens where someone leaves. This cycle can be extremely discouraging for a company. The motivation to keep hiring and training staff can be exhausting. It is tempting to just close doors instead of keeping the hope alive. But as they say, if you've reached the bottom of the barrel, just find a new barrel!

• Personally, my motivation to keep going as before had reached an end. I knew I needed to change, to re-evaluate my approach to business and my work-life balance. There has to be an intentional acknowledgment of the unhealthy work patterns that seem to not affect us when we're younger, but definitely take a toll on our physical, emotional, mental, and spiritual health as we get older. We need to choose to make a sustainable change. It has been said that it's best to work smarter, not harder. Life experiences and each other's stories should recharge us and give us fresh motivation to keep pressing forward healthier and stronger.

• In what area have you lost motivation?

_____

_____

_____

_____

"Discover what is embarrassing or what you are covering up."

• As a company, we have and will always strive to be honest, upfront and fair. If we were ever overpaid on an invoice or paid twice, it was returned. If money was due from us, it was always paid on time. It may seem like a temporary victory to get away with an unfair gain by covering it up, but the truth will always come out. We choose truth.

• I always strive to be honest. I grew up with a hard-working widowed mother (the image of her walking back home carrying wood on her back to keep our chimney going will never leave my mind). Nothing was ever done in my household to cheat anyone else. I come from a culture where truth is often covered up, for the sake of preserving one's pride and honor, but my heart always yearned to be real, honest and open.

• Is there something you have been covering up? It will eventually come to light so it's best to be honest with it upfront with your safe people as soon as possible!

_____

_____

_____

_____

"Realize our trials and failures don't define us."

• BTGI has had its share of trials and failures but it has kept going strong. Our clients have been forgiving of the occasional failure, choosing to see the bigger picture of our years of consistent services. We're so grateful. Since trials and failures do leave a scar, I find myself in team meetings bringing up those events over and over. It's time to stop this mindset and choose to not define myself or BTGI through the lens of the few and far-between mishaps it has had over the years.

• It's hard to forgive yourself over personal failures, but by choosing to not let them define me as a person, I am learning self-forgiveness and stopping the habit of punishing myself over my mistakes.

• Are you defining yourself by a failure?

_____

_____

_____

_____

"Stop doing what we've done out of habit or fear."

• Our biggest habit AND fear has been my wife taking on roles in the company simply out of need or habit. It was the easiest route, and we kept taking it. We found ourselves in a never-ending cycle. We faced the fear of not having the finances to pay for more staff or of them not doing the job correctly. It was difficult to find people who were the right fit and would be willing to stay employed with the company. With my wife, there was no fear of any of that! She loved the company, knew what she was doing, and took everything to heart. By taking a proactive approach, we were able to STOP the cycle once and for all.

• My habit is to go too fast. I always felt like I needed to go fast in America in order to catch up with everyone else who didn't have that initial cultural and language barrier. Eventually, I wanted to pass them all! Plus when you're going fast, you don't feel the bumps in the road, you're just flying over them. I preferred to not feel my bumps. I kept flying over my pain, assuming it would just go away eventually. That was a false hope. Now, I'm choosing to slow down enough in order to STOP this habit. I need to feel the bumps and process each one of them. This was my "winter" to change with the accountability and support I've put in place.

• What habit do you need to STOP?

_____

_____

_____

_____

"Remove distractions during this season."

• BTGI was intentional to place items in the "parking lot" for the time being until we worked through our foundational pillars. It's not easy to set things aside, but we know it's key to work on the most important things without allowing distractions.

• Personally, I committed to say "no" to just about everything this season in order to focus on my own foundational pillars. It's incredibly easy to unknowingly avoid the hard work of inner well-being by staying busy. We're typically distracted by good things. Most requests are disguised with goodness. They may be good, but just not good for me at the time. I need to trust my gut regarding what is best for me at any given season.

• Is there a distraction you continue to say "yes" to in order to avoid something else?

_____

_____

_____

_____

"Look for a rebirth."

• BTGI went through several rebirths and in 2022 went through another one. It's ok to rebirth, rebrand, redefine, and refocus. Times change, so we must also change. The company vision and goals may also change too. It's alright to continue evolving the business into what's currently relevant and needed.

• I too have had a handful of rebirths. When I moved from my hometown to the capital city, when I moved to America, and when I met and married Emily. Later, I intentionally sought a rebirth of my soul.

• Is there an area in your business or personal life that is in need of a rebirth?

_____

_____

_____

_____

"Study yourself."

• We've been working on paving the way forward for BTGI. Our weekly meetings are intentional in dissecting our opportunities and determining whether they're a good fit for us. In studying ourselves, our resources, and what areas we excel in, we make better business decisions for collaboration.

• I often answer my wife with the expression "I don't know why!" I didn't know why I reacted a certain way, said a certain thing, or made a certain decision. Some reasons may be obvious, but some others are not. It's worth investing time by asking why we did what we did and continue in that state of investigating and studying until we reach an answer.

• What area do you need to study about yourself?

_____

_____

_____

_____

"Train for the success. Train for failure."

• As a company, we try to always put forth our Plan A. However, we try to have a Plan B close behind. It's natural to become used to successes and forget about preparing for the worst-case scenario. We may have the perfect interpreter lined up for a certain service who at the very last minute has to call in sick. Time to rapidly employ Plan B! Preparing or training for both the good and worst case scenarios is wise. We try to always keep it in mind.

• As a martial artist, I'm wired to prepare for the worst-case scenario. I'm passionate about self-defense practices and always being aware of my surroundings. I try to have tools in place to "dispatch" when needed. It's not about having a fearful mindset, but about having a prepared mindset. I must be prepared for the best, yet ready for the worst.

• Have you gotten so relaxed that you have forgotten to prepare for a possible catastrophe?

_____

_____

_____

_____

"Grant yourself permission to stop."

• As a company, we needed to slow down to analyze and recalibrate so we could grow stronger than ever. Everyone on the team had permission to slow down to learn and grow.

• I had no outside expectations. My wife encouraged and supported me in taking a sabbatical in order to stop, process, and heal. It was time I granted myself that permission too.

• What do you need to choose to put a complete stop on?

_____

_____

_____

_____

"Recognize patterns."

• Unfortunately, we sometimes accepted assignments solely for the revenue opportunity and not because they align with our company's values. We broke away from the most consistent temptations of these sorts, and are being intentional about implementing the same courage on the one-off offers that seem highly lucrative but may not line up with our best practices.

• The blessing of marriage is having a constant witness to your life and behaviors. My wife has seen me at my best and at my worst. Therefore, she can pick up on my behavioral patterns more quickly than I can. It's not fun to hear them, but I'm thankful for them. Often, it's necessary to hear if we want to address it and correct it.

• Is there a pattern you need to put to rest?

_____

_____

_____

_____

"Lean in, explore, and study the situation. Learn to be present and pay attention."

• As a team, we try to really listen and pay attention to each other's victories and difficulties. We then try to process and encourage each other until the specific team member reaches a solution. By leaning on each other, we create a safe and growth-oriented environment where everyone is working from their sweet spot.

• We are a strengths-based firm. You might ask, what does that mean? One of the most rewarding aspects of teamwork is when each member of the team is able to engage and contribute through the utilization of their strengths. Often we focus on improving our weaknesses, which has a minimal ROI[1]. While continuous improvement is important, we achieve our most significant ROI through the improvement and consistent recalibration to our strengths. This is the key to success! When we engage our strengths, as an organization, or are part of a team that focuses on strengths, greater heights are reached, and we, as individuals, are more satisfied and fulfilled. If you are uncertain of your strengths, this is where we can help!

• It's extremely difficult to quiet me enough to listen and be truly present. I'm a competitor, a doer, and a fixer. I want to support and hear the problems, so I can present a solution, encourage it to be implemented right away and move on! It is difficult to turn off these natural tendencies to truly listen. I understand others are not always wanting to hear a solution, but they simply need a hearing ear. I have my work cut out for me!

• Where do you need to make an effort to be more present?

_____

_____

_____

_____

"Give compassion and acceptance to ourselves in the midst of our struggle."

• It's easy to "talk the talk" before or after a struggle. Being present during the struggle is a different story. We all have expectations for ourselves and our performance during the midst of a struggle that can be unrealistic. Take heed! We need to make sure and STAY encouraged in the midst of trials. Our team needs to continue cheering us on and giving us the lifeline needed to press through the problem. Others need to know they can lean on us if needed.

• The more struggles I go through, the easier it's becoming to give myself grace. It hasn't helped me to blame myself, so it's best to grant myself the same compassion I would give to others.

• Are you being compassionate enough with yourself in order to keep going?

"Accept the gift of Winter."

• As a company we fully embraced our season of Winter. We wanted to use it to shed all of our dead weight and look forward to the next season bringing forth plenty of healthy, vibrant growth.

• Mother Nature knows best, and she's never in a hurry. It takes time to give birth, grow, mature, prune, and then restore. Each season has its value. I want to apply the lessons of Winter and accept the unique gift each one brings. I especially value the gift of rest.

• Can you accept and apply Mother Nature's lessons and gifts —especially the one of rest?

_____

_____

_____

"Remind ourselves of the difficult times we've made it through."

• It's definitely human nature to remember the struggles without their respective victories. As a company, we make it a point to remember and review the year's victories. We write them down so we don't forget where we have been!

• It seems like I've been struggling since I left my hometown. Writing this book has served me as a reminder. It has encouraged me to remember the difficult times I've encountered. I'm grateful for my endurance and the lessons I've learned along the way.

• What is a recent victory or struggle you've had? Have you written it down so you don't forget?

_____

_____

_____

_____

"Remind ourselves that if one or more areas of our lives is in Winter we don't have to despair."

• BTGI intentionally went through a "Winter" season. Afterwards came the time to "Spring" into action!

• I, too, fully embraced the "Winter" as a time for valuable cleansing and preparation for the future.

• Are you Wintering in any area of your life?

"Compartmentalize in a healthy way."

• In our business, it's easy to keep each department compartmentalized. Where it is more challenging is to compartmentalize the pain of past experiences with current situations. Although we can learn from the past, we don't have to keep bringing it up as we move forward.

• I need to learn this skill better. As a business owner, there tend to be little to no boundaries between my work and personal life. Compartmentalizing the business and its struggles from my personal life will allow my brain to be disciplined. It will help me focus on and be more present with my wife.

• Is there something in your life that's bleeding into a category where it doesn't belong?

_____

_____

_____

_____

I encourage you to take this chapter to heart and choose to examine your winter season with purpose and intentionality. As Ralph Waldo Emersen wrote, "Mother Nature has her own pace and her secret is patience. Be patient with yourself, pace yourself, and find and learn the tools and resources necessary in order to be ready to "spring" into action in the next season of your life. Respect and honor each season for they all have something to teach us."

SECTION FOUR: EMPATHY (BE UNDERSTANDING; OF YOURSELF AND OTHERS)

SHARING YOUR GIFT

CHAPTER 13
REDEFINING "HOME"

> *To meditate means to go home to yourself. Then you know how to take care of the things that are happening inside you, and you know how to take care of the things that happen around you. —Thich Nhat Hanh*

ome is a very powerful word for me and one that can mean several different things. Home has several grammatical forms too, depending upon its use, it can be used as a noun, adjective, adverb, and verb! To some, home means buying an elaborate and magnificent house (I once thought that!). For others, it means the city, state, and country of where they were born and raised. Home can also be simply associated with wherever you're living at the time. I have the hardest time embracing this definition as I have laid my head down to rest in numerous countries, and countless places, and I never considered them to be home. However, it may be exactly how you, dear reader, define home. We have explored the different meanings of *home* in my life, and as I continue to progress through my journey, I've seen that:

Home is that place or person or memory where you first felt truly safe and connected, therefore solidifying where you need to "go" to reconnect with your roots and recalibrate.

For me it was *Ommi* and my mountain. *Ommi* will always kiss me endlessly when she first sees me and cry profusely when she has to say goodbye. There is nothing I can do or say to make her stop loving and supporting me. Her face full of unconditional love is ingrained in my being.

And my mountain, which seems to retain the memories of my footprints and welcomes me back whenever I return. For me, the initial steps away from the neighborhood, when I begin the climb up my mountain, can have a bit of uncertainty and confusion. Then, about 500 meters up, you take a turn and everything becomes silent. It's just me and my mountain. I am comforted, and I begin to renew and heal with each step. I feel free, and time completely stops. I'm home. Nothing distracts me. An occasional stray dog may appear in my path, but I just keep moving; wolves, and wild pigs don't stop me either. I'm connected and empowered running up my mountain that I have no doubt I can win any battles thrown at me. There's value in being alone and connecting with nature and allowing her to heal me from the inside out.

Home is your permanent place to store your earthly treasures and lay your head down on your own pillow.

From the day I left my home in Ain Draham, I have been roaming from place to place, laying my head down to rest in over thirty different homes. At times my possessions have been few and a simple backpack was sufficient to contain them, or when I had a little more, I was fortunate to store them away in a friend's basement or garage, or rented a storage unit or locked them up in a trailer attached to my car. The first time I was able to have all of my possessions in one place was when Emily and I got married and bought our first home together. To know that my things weren't scattered all over the place was a moment of pure joy. It is a feeling that is difficult to describe, and one that I look forward to helping others achieve.

Home is where you recover and help each other grow stronger mentally, emotionally, physically, spiritually and socially.

My tank was empty when Emily and I got married but through the comfort of our home, I have started to heal and grow as an individual and as a partner. We have set up areas in the house that help us achieve our goals in these five pillars of health.

 I always wanted to have my own home and now that I have it, I feel a sense of responsibility and privilege to run it well. Each family member living inside my walls is fully supported with space and the ability to grow. I even feel that way about my pets and my plants!

For mental growth, I set up a library with all of our books in one place. I've designed its surroundings with comfortable places to sit, read and relax.

Emotional health is nurtured through cooking, either together or on our own. We intentionally set up our kitchen with all the tools we enjoy in order for it to be a place we look forward to going to and recharging our batteries.

We invested in a home gym to promote physical health. We designed it in such a way that there is space for intense cardio as well as strength training and stretching. Our favorite quotes and athletes are on the walls and we love spending time there!

For our social times, we redesigned our dining space allowing for a more open floor plan. The redesign allows a better flow of guests through the dining and living rooms. We have nooks for being one-on-one with a friend, a four-top when we're enjoying another couple or larger dining tables for six or ten.

For spiritual growth, Nabil's favorite room is what we call our cabin room. It's the only room in our home with a TV and it's designed to look and feel like the inside of a log cabin. My personal space is actually my closet! Sounds strange, but the previous owner of our home built a beautiful basement closet in the master bathroom. They even put in a spiral staircase to go up and down.

I encourage you to make sure you are building your home in a way that these five pillars of health are available on a daily basis to those you dwell with. Proverbs says that "A wise woman builds her home..." which needs to begin with making sure we're "building" the home within ourselves and then we can build up the outward home we've been entrusted with.

Home is where you are welcomed with open arms despite your successes or failures of the day.

This is perhaps the most needed definition of home. We all need a judgment-free zone where we can be "kissed endlessly" no matter what. To be greeted by a spouse after a long day is one of life's greatest blessings! However, what if you choose not to be with a spouse, or you have not found the right person? What then, are you destined for something less than? Of course not! Each of us has a duty to be our own best friend, one that accepts us when we stumble, and one that cheers us on when we cross the finish line. Accept yourself with open arms at the end of the day.

Home is a united family, the assuredness that they have each other's back no matter what.

Abraham Lincoln, in his House Divided speech, stated that "a house divided against itself cannot stand."

A divided home can feel like living with the enemy. I have slept in plenty of homes where this was the case. I've always wished for a home where we were all united, on the same side, and supporting each other as we take on challenges together. This doesn't come naturally or easily, but with open, honest and consistent communication, a united front can be achieved.

Home should not be your chicken exit, don't use it to hide or run away from problems or challenges.

This is at the core of my being and the underlying motto of my life. I never used *home* as an escape. When it's finally time to go home, it's because you gave it your all despite any fears or insecurities and are proud of your results. "Going home" for the wrong reasons will not make the situation go away. You must eventually face it. The longer it takes you to do so, the harder it will be. Don't be afraid. Face it head-on, then *go home* in peace knowing you did your best!

Home is reaching that true level of peace within, of knowing, accepting, forgiving and loving yourself unconditionally and having the confidence of living out your calling on a daily basis.

This is the last definition, and what I desire to fully realize. It is also what I believe is the most pure definition of home. To be our own safest person is what I want. Kripalvananda's opening stanza from one of his poems states, "My beloved child, break your heart no longer. Each time you judge yourself, you break your own heart." Being alone on my mountain helps me look within, see and accept my weaknesses, and celebrate my strengths. It helps me accept the pain. Although we appear strong on the exterior, we may be weak inside. Spending time in meditation will truly lead us home. Being in a place that helps me tune everything else out gives me the capacity to look within, see myself, forgive myself, accept myself and love myself. It may sound odd to state it this way, but it's crucial if we desire inner well being and strength.

Meditating on passages, books I have read, or phrases and quotes that I have heard and love, are key in this process too. Each culture has its own version of how to define home, and for each version there is a danger of becoming unbalanced. Some want to hold you to just their definition of home. For those of us that have flown away from our birth country, the more we see makes us continue to adapt our definitions to encompass how we are evolving and truly feeling about home. For *Ommi*, she was born and raised in a town 20 km from Ain Draham where she married, raised a family, and resides today. For her then, Ain Draham is home in all senses of the word! So how can two very different concepts of home relate to each other when we're together? She sees me as her son who she raised, but I no longer think, talk or act the same. As time goes on, it gets harder to connect naturally, so I have to be intentional about taking time to dig deep within myself, readjust so we can truly experience being "home" together.

I developed vitiligo in my hands shortly after my return from a few weeks in a training institute in the deserts of Nevada in 2012. I was trying to release my extreme pain and stress and it manifested itself physically through my hands. I value hardships and the lessons we can learn from them, but when they leave tangible scars, especially such visible ones, it's a little more difficult for me to accept.

I am a warrior and want to overcome or fix all obstacles, and this is one thing I cannot fix or reverse. I confess being embarrassed by it and the questions I receive about it, but I am building up my courage to not just show my hands freely to the world, but to be proud of them. Our bodies can only take so much beating (inwardly and outwardly) before it starts sending us a message to change course. This was my body telling me enough was enough. Do you have a scar you may or may not be proud of, yet? Try to reassign meaning and value to that scar by focusing on what it can positively teach you about life, instead of the pain it once represented.

CHAPTER 14

RECONCILING "ROOTS" & "WINGS"

 If you know where you are from, it is harder for people to stop you where you are going. —Matshona Dhliwayo

How can our roots and wings live in harmony within us when the two seem to have ended up on opposite sides of the ocean? There is much to love about my birth country. I love my family, neighbors, friends and the sense of community that exists. I can walk into my local coffee shop and everyone greets you laughing, talking and sipping on mint tea. In America, I walk into a coffee shop and see individual people sitting at their own tables. Occasionally, a table has two people sitting together, but they don't look up to greet you as you walk in the door. It's hard for me to reconcile these two different experiences, especially when my heart longs for community. But instead of resenting the American way, I try to take a little piece of my hometown culture with me everywhere. When I walk into a coffee shop, no matter where I'm blessed to be in the world at the time, I greet everyone along my path towards the barista counter. Once I'm in line, I'll strike up a conversation with other patrons and the barista taking my order. I refer to them by name. I'm never met with resistance and I usually turn frowns into smiles by the end of our chat.

Hospitality looks different in America too. Homes are very private. In Tunisia, as soon as you meet someone, you are immediately invited to their house for a meal. Afterward, it is customary to then invite them to your home. We rarely go out to restaurants. The concept of going out to eat is foreign to them. In America, almost every get-together is scheduled at a restaurant rather than at home. I didn't understand this in the beginning. I loved meeting with my friends and family at home! I also often struggle that a reciprocal invitation never happens. I have to make a very conscious choice every single time to not be offended. It is just a completely different perspective on hospitality and the meaning of home.

I remember when I first arrived watching people pull into their garages. That was it. You didn't see them again until the next day. Why was no one out talking to neighbors? I couldn't believe it. As a homeowner and neighbor now, I pull into my driveway, greet and talk with my neighbors, get my mail, take a stroll around the house, then finally get back in my car to pull into the garage. I don't want to miss out on greeting anyone. I want to be an encouragement and portray an open house just as the one I grew up in.

The concept of food is also very different. Years ago, I made a Tunisian couscous from scratch for a lunch gathering after a Sunday morning service. There was one other Tunisian living in Kansas City at the time, who happened to be a chef with his own restaurant. I asked him to help me prepare the dish. We shopped for the best organic ingredients and bought the best quality of lamb meat. Then, we worked all day preparing the dish at his apartment. I decorated the plate like we would back home and sealed it very nicely. I was excited to offer it to the group the next day. By the time we were ready to eat, I explained the dish and its ingredients. I talked about the preparation process so there wouldn't be any fear. Only a handful of people ate from my dish. Food is how we communicate everything in my culture—gratefulness, love, appreciation, acceptance, belonging, family, joy, and comfort. I felt rejected, the exact opposite of the emotions I was accustomed to receiving. At that moment in the building's kitchen, I wanted to disappear. I couldn't wait for everyone to leave so I could throw it all away. I didn't understand their rejection or cultural response to my offer. I took the pain to heart. I know now it wasn't personal, but how was I supposed to reconcile my feelings? Food is a very big deal–almost a culture of its own. It is the vehicle for connecting with others. I still haven't found any better way to connect. The issue then comes down to a choice. I choose to not to take it personally when I'm met with a reaction opposite of my expectation. Just because MY definition of connection happens at the dinner table doesn't mean that's true for everyone. I grew up eating breakfast, lunch and dinner together. I loved meal times. But if you didn't grow up that way, then connecting may happen through other means. If we have empathy towards one another, then we may discover that the *vehicle* used for connecting with one another is far less important than we think.

If we choose to be open to different perspectives, we are broadening our experiences, and doing ourselves a great service at the same time. How so? We're enriching our lives, deepening our worldviews, and becoming more humble and tolerant human beings. I could list everything I love and hate about both, but what is the point in doing that? It will only lead to resentment. Instead, adapt and learn to live in harmony with both. Some call this concept a "third culture." This can be especially true in the children of immigrants that find themselves growing up in two different worlds–the one they're living out at school and the one they come home to.

We have a decision to make. We can forget our roots when we move away and completely adapt to a new culture. Or, we can choose to isolate ourselves all together and create a mini version of our origins. Or, we can choose a perhaps less precise and potentially more challenging path to living in harmony with both cultures. This choice can cause hurt, and lead to misunderstandings and resentments. However, if you learn skills such as forgiveness and empathy, it will give you the most authentic and sustainable connection with your neighbor. In the first two scenarios, we're pulling into the garage and closing the door right behind us on one culture. Our third scenario breeds true community and blesses you with a richer sense of humanity. Just imagine, you can now navigate two very different languages and cultures. You've discovered there are many ways to approach the same end goal. You can pick and choose your favorite traditions from both cultures and celebrate them! I had never heard of St. Patrick's Day, but arriving in America during this celebration made me love it. Since Mother's Day is different in America, Tunisia, and Costa Rica, we celebrate ALL three dates in our home! Choose to be intentional and communicate clearly how you will achieve harmony instead of isolation.

~

" I'm your textbook "third culture kid."[1] I was born in Iceland with a Costa Rican mother and American father. These two worlds were maintained in my home no matter where we lived! By the time I was a teenager though, my family permanently settled in Kansas City and I was faced with choosing for myself which culture I wanted to fully live out - was I a latina or a gringa? I leaned toward my "brown" side more due to some pain from my "white" side, but when I learned and understood what forgiveness meant in my early twenties, my love for my "white" side seemed to come flooding back! There's always going to be a resentment behind your choice of rejecting either culture. You may have been made fun of because of your accent, attire, or appearance so you start hating the culture of which that particular offender poked fun. It may have gotten difficult to keep explaining your perspective so you conform to the majority culture around you. The most prevalent example in trying to maintain two languages is that the majority will give in and revert to one, typically English. Without your mother tongue, you're losing a big part of your roots. I encourage you to stay the course.

In my household growing up, the lines were drawn based on the person, mom=Spanish and dad=English. It IS possible to try a different approach. Please don't give up. You won't regret speaking your mother tongue nor getting and keeping your roots closer. It may lead you to incredible open doors in your future as an interpreter!

CHAPTER 15
REIMAGINING "SUCCESS"

 Success is not the key to happiness. Happiness is the key to success. If you love what you are doing, you will be successful. —Albert Schweitzer

Success has meant many things to me, in Ain Draham it ranged from saving up enough money to buy a pack of Chocotoms, to renting my soccer ball, or negotiating my first sale. My pursuit of success was self-driven when I was younger. I was a natural born competitor. If someone was doing something I loved, I would try to do it better. Once in Tunis, my pursuit of success became one of survival. I was so driven that I was able to surpass, not just survive. Once in America, it was about finding success in the land reputedly flowing with milk and honey. I achieved success in my home country with relatively few scars, so why wouldn't I be able to succeed in this foreign land? I needed to prove that I could make it. A validation mark from my culture that I was a successful American. My drive was for the approval of others without giving it much thought for myself. I worked tirelessly in all of my classes at school–never missing a class, never being late. I would often fall asleep in the library studying. I was a stellar employee too, always working harder than the rest and getting ahead.

My drive for success never ceased and seemed to get miraculously refueled each day. Two years after leaving home, I hadn't made "it" yet. After five, eight, and even ten years, I still hadn't achieved my dream. With each year that passed, I felt further and further away from achieving cultural success and more embarrassed of how long it was taking me. By the tenth year, I did go back home for a month, but I had returned without the tangible evidence that I had attained the respected validation marks, proving once and for all that I had made something of myself. I was discouraged, hurt and felt an extreme sense of being misunderstood. Over the next decade, I traveled back to Ain Draham two more times. I was in a better place financially each time, but I still was not quite at the expected standard.

Would I ever be able to reach the standard? I felt like the goal line kept moving further away as soon as I approached it. There were faces of disappointment back home. Was it even possible to win at the game of "success" under these rules? I realized I needed to define success for myself and not for the sake of meeting an arbitrary standard. I wanted to be independent from these endless expectations. I needed to analyze my own personal goals and invest my drive toward reaching them. Success is living in the intersection of the Venn diagram; that area that overlaps what you love and your gifts. How many times have you found yourself in the flow, grinding away for no reason other than you enjoyed it? Giddy with your work, even in the absence of others noticing. Perhaps you've seen it on the face of a chef cooking an award-winning dish or a gardener tending to their incredible blooms. I'm happiest when practicing my kata alone in the backyard. Being able to live in that intersection of loving what I do and my gifts is my definition of success. My gift for sales led me to a love of interpreting. That led to a love of cultures and coaching to prevent cultural misunderstandings and hardships. Besides my karate, my sweet spot lies in helping you, and others, make it through our journeys a little better. We're not meant to struggle through life alone.

We need to strive to reach our own personal definition of success. When it comes to cultural expectations, we'll never win. Unfortunately, those expectations will never go away, but that doesn't mean we walk away from them forever. My desire is for us to be confident and believe in our own personal successes. Doing so will equip us with tools on how to handle the pressure of unmet expectations. I humbly ask for permission to allow me the honor of helping you achieve success from cultural pressures and expectations, regardless of when, or how you arrived at the current place in your journey.

This fifty year journey has been hard and my path was "recalculated" many, many times. But, since I believe in embracing the tour AND the detour, I have kept going, and going, and going. Then suddenly, my trusty Garmin declared, "You have arrived!" I was finally home.

Home is still with *Ommi*. I continue to travel yearly to be with her and build *her* home back up, helping now to lift her head up high among her neighbors and family members.

I attached a little studio space to her home that overlooks *my* mountain for her to enjoy the scenery while I'm away and for my wife and I to have a place to lay our heads down when we travel.

I am also now *home* to myself, *home* with all of my earthly possessions, and most importantly, *home* with my beloved wife. I reached my "somewhere" and I KNOW you will too. Keep pressing on and if we can lend a guiding hand, it would be our privilege.

In the 1990's I was a teenager in the U.S., and that meant one thing, Michael Jordan and the Chicago Bulls! I was obsessed with Jordan because it was like watching magic on the court every time he played. I would sit RIGHT in front of the TV so I didn't miss a single move, jump, twist, turn, pass or shot that he would make during the game! He once said "there's no "I" in the word team but there is an "I" in win." His meaning was that he would do his part, regardless. Regardless of what, exactly? If his teammates did their part, all the better, but he would always do his part, because he wanted to win! Michael wanted to win because he had a heart for the game. He loved it! He was going to play no matter what he was facing, be it injury, illness, or the inclement weather that nearly postponed his very first All-Star game. If he had to take up slack, he would play extra hard so his team would still have a chance to win. He even had a "Love of the Game" clause built into his first contract with the Chicago Bulls which gave him the freedom to play whenever and wherever he wanted. This was unheard of! Jordan was living in his sweet spot and is one of the greatest players of all time. That is success.

My other favorite Michael, Michael Phelps, would do in the water what Jordan did on the court every single time! His field of magic was in the pool, and with every stroke your heart pounded in your chest until his fingers grazed the touchpad, sometimes, with only microseconds ahead of his Olympic opponents. He was superhuman because of his love of the sport. He went down in history as the most successful and decorated Olympian of all time, having participated in a total of FIVE

Summer games and winning a total of 28 medals; 23 Gold, 3 Silver and 2 Bronze. That is success.

Nabil once interpreted alone in simultaneous mode[1] for a four-hour board meeting. He did it because his teammate did not show up. He picked up the slack to "win." He got it done, ALONE! How? Why? Because he wanted to win, had a heart for the "sport" and had trained for it! We are capable of SUPERHUMAN acts when we fully engage and train our natural abilities in what we love to do! Success!

So how does success reward an interpreter? We don't perform in basketball courts or swimming pools with cheering crowds all around, but in soundproof booths filled with microphones. Typically we are in a concealed location, out of the public eye, and away from the noise of the event. No one really knows we're there! Jordan and Phelps had the eyes of the whole world on them when they performed and were rewarded with trophies and medals. Do you know how our trophies and medals appear? They are the look of complete dependance, utter trust, and extreme gratefulness on our client's face. Before they heard our voice through the audio receiver in their ear, they were alone, scared, lost, and confused. However, when we're there with them, they feel heard and understood! This is our gold medal, this is our measure of success!

We get to impact the souls of humankind through our work. We are part of the best game in the world. I encourage you to continue fueling and fanning the flames of fire of your hearts so you can be superhuman in your field. We are leaving a lasting and sustainable impact when we unleash our passion. It is an honor and privilege! HONOR your gift. Train to be the greatest of all time, and you'll be part of history too.

CHAPTER 16
RECALCULATING DESTINATIONS

 Things may come to those who wait, but ONLY the things left by those who hustle. —Abraham Lincoln

Your current destination on your GPS can be changed. As Jim Rohn says, we are not like geese that ONLY fly north and south year after year, we can go in any direction we'd like! Just because you hear the words "you have arrived" does not mean growth "has arrived" too. We can't stay stuck in our mindsets, even when physically we're settled in for the time being. What are you gaining by staying the same? Nothing. If we're not intentionally trying to keep moving forward, we're actually moving backward! I want to do my best to motivate you to recalculate your current destination, mentally or physically or both, but it's up to you and me to actually punch in that new address on the B line and click Start! Sure, easier said than done, especially when we encounter resistance.

What if the weather suddenly changes making the trip harder to take? Will you still drive through the "storm" or go back to bed and wait for a perfectly sunny day? Don't be discouraged or afraid, you must take the risk and start driving, even if it's just for a few miles, you will be further than you were today. Pilots are constantly course-correcting due to unexpected occurrences en route. Don't let the current weather forecast stop you from where you need to go in life or when you should start your journey, *you* dictate your life. Don't let life just happen to you, you *happen* to your life!

It will always be our choice how much we drive each and every day we're gifted with. Push yourself. And remember, this is *your* unique journey. You can, and should, take others with you, but the journey is unique to you. So no comparisons of not being as far ahead as others, or not being the fastest or even the best driver out there. As Dr. Seuss once wrote, "today you are You, that is truer than true. There is no one alive, that is Youer than You!" So, be You, and to someone else, and remember, YOU are the better driver to someone else, so stay encouraged.

I have taken you through my life's journey so far and tried to share my lessons along the way in the spirit of humbly hoping to help you along your way. Let's recap these core values together and highlight the key takeaways:

Core Value: **Fairness.**

Do you understand how to treat *others* with honesty? Have you put a sense of urgency and determination into learning how to manage your life and business from a place of truth and impartiality?

It takes courage to follow the narrow path of honesty. I traveled to America with a valid visa and followed the immigration path to the end without coloring outside of the lines. It was *not* the easy route, especially with the limited hours allowed to work making it near impossible to survive, much less thrive, but it was the right thing to do. I was able to start a business and have the chance to not only continue doing what was right for me but now for others too. I had clients to serve and interpreters to partner with. And I had my marriage to protect most of all, our most sacred human relationship and the one that deserves utmost honesty.

We explored these questions together:

• **Are you willing to count the cost for doing what is right?**

_____

_____

_____

_____

• **Is there something you're not trusting your gut on?**

_____

_____

_____

_____

• Did you leave your past behind too quickly or for the wrong reasons? Could there be a pot of gold waiting for you back there that you hadn't noticed before?

_____

_____

_____

_____

• Are you choosing to "go home" or take the chicken exit on something you know in your gut you should go for?

_____

_____

_____

_____

• Is there an area that you need to take through a "winter" season?

_____

_____

_____

_____

CORE VALUE: **Empathy.**

Do you understand how to put yourself in *other* people's shoes? Have you put a sense of urgency and determination into learning how to be truly understanding of another?

I struggled with truly finding and defining *home* for myself for decades after leaving my birth home. I struggled with how to keep my roots and wings living together in harmony in my heart. Who was I and how was *I* going to define what success meant for me? Based on these personal struggles and all the ones we've witnessed our beloved international community go through, we desired to put ourselves in *their shoes* and as a team at BTGI have developed a cultural training program to help bridge that gap between roots and wings. We are offering our tools and resources through this program so we may take advantage of learning and growing together. The cultural struggles don't just affect us while we're living in our passport country, but when we travel to visit our birth country too. It would be an honor to take the journey back home with you, while you prepare to travel back, while you are on the ground, and as you prepare to leave and re-enter. It's important to analyze the state of the five pillars of health we discussed: mentally, emotionally, physically, spiritually and socially before traveling, so we don't take any extra "baggage" on our already difficult journey ahead of us. Let's be honest with ourselves, we've changed and no longer "fit in" when we travel back home. We at BTGI know this and want you to know you're heard and understood. Let's partner together and discuss how you can eventually feel empowered about:

• Home: what does it truly mean to you?

_____

_____

_____

_____

• Roots and Wings: are they living in harmony within you?

_____

_____

_____

_____

• Success: have you taken the time to be truly at peace with yourself and your accomplishments?

_____

_____

_____

_____

CORE VALUE: **Enrichment.**

Do you understand *you* can add value? Have you put a sense of urgency and determination into personal growth to continue adding value to yourself and others?

I knew getting a driver's license even without owning a car would be of value to me one day. Getting my sales and marketing degree and going to language school to learn English were also going to be of value. I didn't know my *why* before taking these steps, I just knew that they would serve me later. In this section, we asked you:

• **Have closed doors for growth opportunities worn you down to the point that you stopped knocking?**

_____

_____

_____

_____

• **Have you identified your strengths? Are you intentional about engaging your strengths?**

_____

_____

_____

_____

• **Will you sacrifice whatever it takes, even personal comfort and stability, for the sake of growth?**

_____

_____

_____

_____

• **Does your gut keep nudging you to move on but you've been ignoring it?**

_____

_____

_____

_____

And finally . . .

CORE VALUE: **Drive.**

Do you understand *you* were born with a gift? Have you put a sense of urgency and determination into discovering and implementing it?

Just as I was born a salesman and instinctively put it into practice through the renting of my soccer ball and bicycle and then the selling of my quickly multiplying rabbits, you were born with a gift too. My desire through each chapter in this book is for you to say "me too" and not "so what," because it's not just about what my story has taught me, but what it can teach us all. We asked you:

• How can you turn your gift into a skill?

_____

_____

_____

_____

• Do you need to aim higher than the geographical area you've been focused on?

_____

_____

_____

_____

• Is your love of something reason enough for you to start a business venture about it?

_____

_____

_____

_____

There is no wrong time to do the right thing. Start. And if you already started, keep going no matter what. Don't give up. Sam Parker states that:

"At 211°F, water is hot. At 212°F, it boils. And with boiling water, comes steam…and with steam, you can power a train. One degree. Applying one extra degree of temperature to water means the difference between something that is simply very hot and something that generates enough force to power a machine. 211°F can serve a purpose but 212°F is the extra degree – the extra degree that will bring exponential results – exponential results to you and those you touch throughout your days."

You very well might be just ONE degree away from exponential results, so don't dare take the chicken exit now!

SECTION FIVE: FEED (FAIRNESS, EMPATHY, ENRICHMENT, DRIVE)

AT OUR
CORE...

Our values reflect who we are, why we do what we do, and how we do it. We bridge gaps. We build ramps. We strengthen businesses, communities, and the lives of others. Our values, when shortened, spell FEED. It is how we conduct ourselves as a firm, as a group, and as people:

FAIRNESS
- Everyone deserves to be understood. Our solutions provide the necessary catalyst to promote and achieve equity.

EMPATHY
- Seek to understand, is the first step toward creating a better world, and our solutions begin and end with this tenet.

ENRICHMENT
- Providing the highest value, and quality is a given, yet we strive to go further, and we do so by offering substance without expectation in return.

DRIVE
- Action makes no guarantees, but inaction guarantees nothing. Thus, we strive, we try, and we endeavor, in all we offer, and all that we do.

Bridging the Gap
INTERPRETING

913-952-3739
www.kansascityinterpreting.com

CHAPTER 17
TO THE CORE

CONTRIBUTED BY RICHARD MOREHOUSE

Throughout our time together, there have been recurring themes surrounding a set of core values. What are core values?[1] These are the internal traits and qualities that reflect deeply held beliefs.They are the driving forces intuitively accessed when a decision is made. Values such as these cannot be clawed away from who we are, and it is these values that have been integral to Nabil's journey. They are his personal, individual values, and they are the values that propel BTGI. It is possible you too may share one, perhaps even two; however, it would be rare that you or your business would share them all. Similar to fingerprints, a primary set of core values are unique differentiators. Core values are inherent, but they can be used as a tool for success. How, you might ask? The identification of core values is a simple concept to understand, but they are not easily unearthed. Before we explore how to identify core values, here are three primary considerations:

1. Aspirations are not core values.

Each of us aspires to be something, perhaps it is something more, or it may be something different. Stated differently, aspirations are our hopes, ambitions, and goals. The main difference between aspirations and core values is change. Aspirations can change, but core values do not. Here's the thing, to be our most effective, we need both, right? Identifying your core values in relation to your aspirations ensures that you are aligned with your true, "hold dearly" beliefs. Doing so means that you will be far less apt to set goals antithetical to your core, or aspire to be something that you are not.

2. Pay-to-play requirements are not core values, unless . . .

What is meant by "pay-to-play"? This statement reflects the price of admission, be it the price for our lives, or our business. A perfect example of pay-to-play in life is the critical act of breathing. How often do you consider your breath? If you are like most, not very often, but if you stop breathing, well then, everything else becomes moot. The point is this, core values are not "pay-to-play". Another example would be honesty as a core value. Now, some might declare they are never dishonest, and therefore honesty is a core value. This would mean that even small, white lies, such as if you were running late to a meeting and you tell your client, "I am only five minutes away", knowing full well you are actually eleven minutes away. Of course, we all strive to be honest, and trustworthy, right? To be a core value, however, means that honesty is an absolute.

3. Core values are guiding behaviors from top to bottom.

Core values guide your behaviors in everything that you do. In business, core values guide the organizational decisions, they are reflected within the leadership, staff, suppliers, partners, and even the firm's customers. These guiding behaviors are not only the drivers, but they are guardrails. When an individual or a business is not in alignment it is apparent and visible. What does this look like? When the energy giant Enron collapsed and ultimately failed, one of the firm's listed core values was Integrity. Integrity is defined as a whole, undivided, and moral. Due to the fact that 21 people were convicted of wrongdoing, and 85,000 employees (Cohn, 2019) associated with Enron's auditing company lost their jobs as a result of decisions made by the firm's leadership, it is clear that their core values were not guiding behaviors.

How are core values identified? As we discussed earlier, the process is simple, but far from easy. In fact, most of us have never conducted a core value exercise, so the first step is under-standing, you are not alone! To help you on this journey of discovery, the following are three steps that will help get you started:

1. Reflect upon your peaks

When were you at your happiest? What was happening at the time, and what factors led to this instance? Detailing the elements of this event, or events, is a great way to begin the process of identifying what is most important to you. Humans connect through stories, so one of the easiest methods to use for this reflection exercise, or, if you have trouble getting started, would be to tell a friend or family member the story of when you were happiest. Asking them to listen and take notes, writing specific words or descriptors that you use. Afterwards, review the list and circle words that elicit an emotional response.

2. Admiration

Who do you admire? Listing family, friends, co-workers, fictional characters, or famous people (present, or historical), is an eye-opening exercise, but do not stop there! For each name, list the traits that you admire about them. Afterwards, review the list and circle the traits that elicit an emotional response.

3. List

This option is number three on the list, because it requires less work, but used correctly, it can result in exceptional outcomes. Using your favorite web browser, conduct a search for a list of words. Be aware that there are many such lists, some are nouns, some are verbs, and everything in between. Furthermore, you will have resources ranging from just a few words, to thousands of words! This means that you might end up with so many words to choose from that you will just end up choosing words that resonate with you so that you can quit the exercise. Again, the list process is not a bad choice, but it can be overwhelming. If you decide to use this direction, the following is a list of 48 words to help get you started:

Authenticity	Caring	Fairness	Health
Achievement	Challenge	Faith	Humor
Adventure	Citizenship	Family	Influence
Appreciation	Community	Leadership	Justice
Authority	Compassion	Learning	Kindness
Autonomy	Competency	Love	Knowledge
Balance	Contribution	Loyalty	Peace
Boldness	Creativity	Mindfulness	Respect
Determination	Curiosity	Openness	Responsibility
Dependability	Growth	Optimism	Security
Empathy	Happiness	Poise	Service
Abundance	Collaboration	Friendships	Wisdom

After you have conducted your exploration, and have identified words that resonate with you the most clearly, and emotionally, the real work begins. The challenge in front of you is to now reduce your list to the words that connect with you on the deepest of levels. The goal is to pare the list to no fewer than three, with no more than seven. Once this is complete, you are nearing your goal. The next phase is to define your words' meanings. Not necessarily the Webster's Dictionary definitions, but what the word communicates to you! For example, if one of your core values is *Dependability*, how would you define it? What does dependability sound like when you speak the word? How does it affect your decision-making? If dependability is a value, how might it look if you were undependable?

You are now nearing your final push. After defining your three to seven words, don't simply post them on the wall, not yet anyway. Take your words and wear them for a while, just like you might wear a jacket. Try them on, so to speak, and test them in use. We have referred to intuition throughout the book, this is the time to access your intuition, and to conduct a gut check. As you spend time with your words do you find yourself aligning with your priorities? Regularly reflect to answer whether or not your decisions are reflected as it relates to your newly found values. If after fourteen days of trial, and the answer is yes to the above questions, you are now ready to post, and refer to your values. If you have completed this exercise as an individual, or as a business, it is time to share with the world! Perhaps you are wondering, what are the core values of Bridging the Gap Interpreting, well, wonder no more:

AT OUR CORE . . .

Our values reflect who we are, why we do what we do, and how we do it. We bridge gaps, and build ramps, to create, and strengthen bonds in business, communities, and in the lives of individuals. Our values, expressed by the acronym F.E.E.D. are how we conduct ourselves, as a firm, as a group, and as people:

Fairness

Everyone deserves to be understood. Our solutions provide the necessary catalyst to promote and achieve equity.

Empathy

Seek to understand, is the first step toward creating a better world, and our solutions begin and end with this tenet.

Enrichment

Providing the highest value, and quality is a given, yet we strive to go further, and we do so by offering substance without expectation in return. and le

Drive

Action makes no guarantees, but inaction guarantees nothing. Thus, we strive, we endeavor, and try, in all we offer, and in all that we do.

Switching to a business, or firm focus, the identification of core values is just the beginning. Implementation and consistent usage of core values, be it in your decision making, goal setting, or in developing a strategy, is the true test of success. There are three keys to ensure solid, and successful implementation of *your core values. (* be aware, core values are not limited to the firms. This implementation process can be used to implement individuals, couples, and family core values too). They are accomplished by:

1. Heard by all, understood by all

The firm is organized by strategy, divisions, departments, and individuals. When core values are identified, and to be of any use, they must be held and understood. This means when they are heard, or spoken of, accessed and used, that they are understood! Here at BTGI, we are fond of saying "Nothing is better than being Understood."™ This statement refers to our interpreting services, but can also be used as a method of describing how the organization is optimized through the accessing and utilization of core values, which are heard by all, and understood by all.

2. Fundamentals for hiring, firing, promoting and recognition

All organizations consist of individuals, and well-run organizations are made up of those individuals who reflect the firm's core values. This essentially means that the Human Resources department is led by the business's core values. As such, recruiting efforts are informed through the lens of core values. Evaluations, performance, promotions, and even employee separations are conducted with the core values in mind. Just as importantly, promotions, acknowledgment and employee recognition is completed, in concert, with core values.

3. Decision Making

When making decisions, be they long-range, medium, or tactical, the successful firm must appropriately access their core values. The P2P product and design company Threadless, began in 1999. Its mission was to create a community of artists who were supported by like-minded customers. In response to decision-making, and their core values, Threadless states (Threadless, 2023), "We think about these [core] values every day and evaluate our efforts by measuring against them." Beautiful! Such an exacting example of implementing the power of core values within everyday decisions.

As we can see, determining your firm's (or individual) core values is a simple concept, but as we said, the process is not easy. The difference is that you now have a set of tools in your hands that you can use and access at any time. Furthermore, *bridging the gap* is more than just part of our name, it is what we

218

do. As you are working through your core values, if you find the process more challenging than expected, you now have a partner that you can lean on. It is said, "if you want to go fast, go alone, but if you desire to go far, do so as a team." You need not "go it alone", we have the resources and the team that can help you not only achieve your goals but do so confidently and in alignment with your core values!

Citations

Cohn, S. (2019, March 23). *Former Enron CEO Jeffrey Skilling wants back into the energy business.* CNBC. Retrieved January 11, 2023, from https://www.cnbc.com/2019/03/23/former-enron-ceo-jeffrey-skilling-wants-back-into-the-energy-business. html#:~:text=A%20scandal%20for%20the%20ages,employ-ees%20who%20lost%20their%20jobs.

Threadless values. Threadless. (n.d.). Retrieved January 11, 2023, from https://www.threadless.com/values/

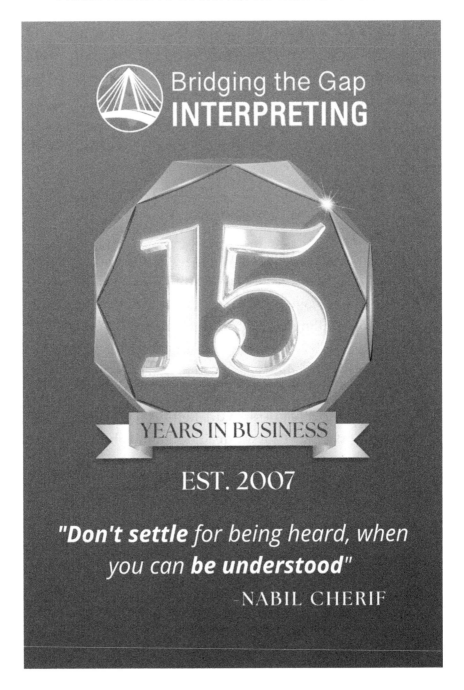

CHAPTER 18
LAGNIAPPE

CONTRIBUTED BY RICHARD
MOREHOUSE

W e have nearly reached the end of our *I Wasn't Born To Go Home* journey. Of course we hope this is just the beginning, but even so, all books must end. However, before we go, we would like to leave you with an additional chapter as a *lagniappe*.[1]

The power of connections is often discussed within our firm, and connections are what all successful organizations need. Bridging the Gap Interpreting celebrated its fifteenth year in business in 2022. The power of connections could not have been displayed more vividly as the firm's interpreters[2], clients, staff, family and friends, new and old, gathered to celebrate Nabil and Emily, and the company they built. This is where BTGI excels, and it is also where we can help you! Whether you are thinking of starting a business, have started, or are celebrating your milestone anniversary, the Small Business Association (shorturl.at/kyY03) reports that America's economy is made up of small businesses. 2019 data from the U.S. Census

Bureau shows a total of 6.1 million employer firms, 99.7% of which are businesses with less than five hundred employees. Astoundingly, firms with fewer than 10 employees make up 78.5% of the U.S. employers! The point of highlighting this data is to acknowledge the significance of America's entrepreneurs. They represent the backbone of the U.S. economy, and one could credibly argue that entrepreneurs also represent the legs on which the economy runs, and the arms embracing the entire system. If you are in this category, well done, you are appreciated! If you are just beginning, you can do it! One of our core values centers on drive, and operating a business is fundamentally a reflection of drive. However, processes and execution are equally as important. In this way, we encourage you to lean on BTGI as a resource, we can help!

Bridging the Gap Interpreting, LLC is a language agency built by interpreters, for interpreters. What exactly does this mean, "for interpreters"? This means as an organization that understands the demands of interpreters, we in turn ensure that we are advocating for interpreters. On one hand, it might mean that we are providing materials in advance of their session so that they can be better prepared for the engagement. However, on the other hand, it means that we have effective empathy for the role that they fill. Interpreters and translators[3] are not machines (well, some translation is conducted via machine), they are 360-degree human beings. They are parents, and spouses. They have children, and siblings. They can become hungry, and can get cold (particularly on those cold mornings and nights heading to sessions). They have times of joy, and extreme sadness. They are individuals with hearts and souls. When we speak of the Heart of the Interpreter™ we are referring to the distinct passion and empathy that interpreters have for what they do. Interpreters may balance their roles, but one thing is consistently immeasurable, their heart. We began celebrating the Heart of the Interpreter in early 2022, with recognition and acknowledgment.

In essence, we recognize that the interpreter's heart is the soul of our firm, and we could not do it without them. Interpreters operate within a strict code of ethics. Code 7.b states: The interpreter performs her or his duties as unobtrusively as possible. To a person, interpreters can often be the one that is least likely to ask for a break, or even a sip of water, even after continuously speaking in another language while listening to a different language. All this to say, interpreters are not machines, they have human qualities, and foibles, just like us. The Heart of the Interpreter is what makes them different from most, and in this way, we celebrate and raise them up to the recognition that they deserve. If you, or someone you know, is an interpreter, we applaud you, and them, and if you would like to connect with an agency built by interpreters, for interpreters, we know a great one!

The bridge that leads from Kansas City to North Kansas City is called the Bond Bridge. Construction was started in 2007, the same year that BTGI was started, and opened to limited traffic in 2010. What makes this bridge so special is not its stunning cable-stayed delta-shaped pylons, which reach nearly 300' into the skies above the Missouri River, or how it was constructed. The foundational difference surrounding the Bond Bridge, according to the architect who designed the bridge, Bradley Townsend, said "it was the first time in Missouri Department of Transportation history that community involvement with such a project was solicited." Townsend went on to say, "the Bond bridge is a manifestation of a community component, acting as a bridge between the community and the transportation department. What a great metaphor!

As with BTGI, the Bond Bridge accessed the strengths of the community and the public transportation department, and the designing architect, Bradley Townsend acted as the interpreter which resulted in the bridge structure represented in the logo for Bridging the Gap Interpreting. Such a beautiful example. Beyond bridging gaps, BTGI also builds ramps, and we do so by strengthening individuals and teams. Much in the same way that we help companies and firms unearth their core values, we do the same by uncovering individual strengths. Strengths are characteristics that each of us innately have and they inform the way that we act and respond. Using a consistent, and scientifically backed set of tools, we are able to identify, develop and enhance each person's Top Five strengths. Strengths-based design creates powerful companies, teams, and individuals, and just like the Bond Bridge was a manifestation, identification of strengths can manifest improved satisfaction, engagement, and ultimately lead to success.

Home as a central theme is throughout every page in *I Wasn't Born To Go Home*, and we are fully committed to helping others not only with their definitions of home, but with their home going experiences. Bridging the Gap Interpreting is foundationally an organization consisting of emigrants who have immigrated to the United States. Of course there are exceptions, but by and large the aspect of leaving one's birth country and ultimately living in America is a consistent story. What is different is the cultures from which they were formed. This is the concept of: home, Home and HOME. BTGI recognizes the dizzying array of challenges when faced with home, Home and HOME. From scheduling conflicts, airfare, culture differences, hero expectations, to fitting in, the entire scope can be overwhelming and stressful. To answer some of these obstacles we are developing a 24/7 accessible curriculum which is easily digestible prior to arriving Home, while at HOME, and upon returning home. The principals are rooted in a clear and personal understanding of the joys and trials of home with a goal of blending home, Home and HOME to become more manageable, and stable.

Here we are. We have made it to the end of our journey together, but this does not mean it is the end entirely. We literally are closing this chapter, but we can absolutely write more, together! As a company, BTGI bridges gaps and builds ramps, and we do this because it is our passion and what we are called to do. At the end of each day, our goal is to have given more than we took, and to help rather than harm. If there is something that we can help you with, be it a word of encouragement, defining your core values, identifying strengths, or helping you return home joyfully, we want to be there for you. You can reach us by:

Website: www.btgi.world

Instagram: _btgi

LAGNIAPPE

Facebook: Bridging the Gap Interpreting

Amazon: https://a.co/d/8nFxMHH

Heart of the Interpreter™: www.heartoti.com

Phone: 913-952-3739

Franchise Information: office@kansascityinterpreting.com

227

AFTERWORD

Writing has been a healing process. It has helped make sense of what has transpired over the years - not to answer the question of "why" or "why me" but to answer the question of "what shall I do with it." Our journey's are all different and believe it or not, even its trials, challenges, obstacles and what we may view as failures *can* be purposeful and meaningful. Not just for us, but for others as well. I've been on a journey of discovery for fifty years now and it has led me to where I am today. I am blessed with a renewed sense of self and bursting with passion to continue pursuing meaning, significance and connectivity with my roots and my wings.

I had been wanting to share my story through the gift of writing for many years. Perhaps the right time is now, after twenty-two years in America, because I just now reached my desired destination of *home*. Being *home* internally through self-acceptance and receiving unconditional love from my wife and externally through the safety of where we lay our head down at night to rest, is the manifestation of success. In order to arrive at that sweet spot of living out our calling, we need to be *home* first. This doesn't mean we finally arrived at perfection, but at an understanding of life's journey and have accumulated enough tools necessary to keep moving forward, and know where to get more when needed! Allow me to help you get more tools in your life so that you too may be *home* to yourself and live in your sweet spot.

—Nabil Cherif

Assisting Nabil in writing his story to share with the world has been an honor. Our writing process was one of a passionate orator dictating to his scribe. Our date nights were replaced with me listening to his stories in my pj's while taking notes in my journal, which led us to more laughs and tears together than any "getting dressed up for a nice dinner and a movie" could have given us! I got to know him better and realized that how he's wired now, is how he's always been wired to be! It was priceless. I will be the first in line to testify to the fact that what he says is what he does, always.

The words in this book are not just motivational words that he doesn't apply to his own life, they *are* his life. In the years we've been married, I have learned to become more coura-geous and focused on possibilities rather than on the "what-ifs" that tend to never happen anyway! Anytime I am afraid or faced with a challenge, I say to myself "I wasn't born to go home" and I take a deep breath and go for it! I don't want fear to have the last say in my life's decisions and even though I *am* scared out of my mind, I'm not taking the chicken exit ever again!

—Emily Cherif

GLOSSARY

1. LE FOOTBALL

1. Resourceful/Resourcefulness: "The defining factor (for success) is never resources, it's resourcefulness." —Tony Robbins. Our resources are what is around us, all the tangible and intangible things - like making a soccer ball out of what I had lying around the house. And our resourcefulness has to do with our creativity in using them - like how I made a soccer ball out of what I found.
2. Obstacles: Something that makes it difficult to do something; an object that you have to go around or over; something that blocks your path.

4. IMPOSSIBLE N'EST PAS FRANÇAIS!

1. Agent de Transit: The profession of transit agent is part of the transport domain. The job of transit agent is very complete. While its primary role is to organize the transport of goods, whether nationally or internationally, it must also manage all administrative formalities related to transport.

12. SLOWING DOWN TO SPEED UP?

1. ROI: Per Investopedia, return on investment is a performance measure used to evaluate the efficiency or profitability of an investment or compare the efficiency of a number of different investments. ROI tries to directly measure the amount of return on a particular investment, relative to the investment's cost.

14. RECONCILING "ROOTS" & "WINGS"

1. Third Culture Kid: Per Psychology Today, individuals who grow up in multiple cultures and countries are called Third Culture Kids (TCK). Children of international educators, missionaries, diplomats, military personnel, and business people are often identified as TCKs. As TCKs grow up, they are thought to synthesize elements of their first and second cultures into a

233

third culture. The third culture refers to a culture that is different from the TCKs' parents' culture (i.e., the first culture is the country of citizenship) and different from the culture in which the TCKs are located (i.e., the second culture being the foreign host country / countries).

15. REIMAGINING "SUCCESS"

1. Simultaneous Mode: Simultaneous interpreting is oral translation parallel with the spoken sentence. The interpreter reproduces what the speaker says while the speaker is still talking, with no delay. In this setting, the interpreter and participants wear headsets.

17. TO THE CORE

1. Core Values: Per Indeed, core values are personal ethics or ideals that guide you when making decisions, building relationships and solving problems. Identifying the values that are meaningful to you can help you develop and achieve personal and professional goals. It can also help you find jobs and companies that align with your ideals.

18. LAGNIAPPE

1. Lagniappe: French word for "something a little extra."
2. Interpreter: Per Kent State University, an interpreter, someone who repeats the message but in a different language, deals with live conversation, which can include translating meetings, conferences, appointments, live TV, and more. Since interpretation is in real time, it requires someone who is able to work under pressure with excellent communication skills.
3. Translator: Per Kent State University, when working within the translation field, one is working to successfully decipher the meaning of written content from a source language into the language that is targeted.

ACKNOWLEDGMENTS

 Passion is the real difference maker; it separates the extraordinary from the ordinary. It leads you to: Believe things you would not have believed. Feel things you would not have felt. Attempt things you would not have attempted. Accomplish things you would not have accomplished. Meet people you would not have met. Motivate people you would not have motivated. Lead people you would not have led. —John C. Maxwell

I had the privilege to meet and shake John Maxwell's hand and chat with him for a bit. I remember those minutes despite the shortness of them and, despite the amount of people that were there, I knew that John, along with his team of Chris, Roddy and Mark truly meant to see me, value me and honor me. Thank you for who you are and your contributions to leadership and growth. I am a proud team member and look forward to running into you in the journey of life.

Next is my personal tribe. Some are my family, some are people I would not have met if it weren't for my drive fueled by passion to keep moving forward. I will do my best to honor each one of you here in writing, or in person as soon as I get the chance!

I would like to go back to the very beginning and thank *Ommi* again, who has a sacred place in my heart for all of her sacrifices and gifts to us all, specifically me.

I would like to thank all my brothers and sisters, especially my two sisters, Samira and Wahida, for all that they did to help raise me. They all continue to contribute, directly or indirectly, to my growth and development. I was the youngest and got all the benefits of love and care despite the hard life sometimes.

I would like to thank their children, my beloved nieces and nephews, who were born while I still lived in Tunisia and those who were born after I left. Some of you I have met, some I have not met yet, but I am a proud uncle to ALL of you and hope to be a good example for you to follow! My love to: Sami, Salim, Dhouha, Najla, Jamel, Imen, Aymen, Skander, Aya, Sawssan, Jihed, Manel, Dua, Ghassen, Ghada, Nassim, Hamma, Azza, Azmi, Samar and Maram. There are three more from a brother I haven't had the privilege to meet yet, nor his three children, but hope to one day!

I would like to thank my previous teachers in my primary school and secondary school, the majority of them were so caring and serving.

I would like to thank my mentors who I learned a lot from through direct support or through books I had the privilege to read in my three languages.

I would like to thank my first American friends in Tunisia, Tim, Charles and John, with whom I had the chance to practice and enhance my English and learn firsthand about American culture.

I would like to thank my friend Steve and his family for all the help and support they gave me when I first arrived in America, through helping with a dentist cleaning, all the food they fed me, and all the late night conversations we had that made such a difference in my life.

I would like to thank my dear friend Brian and his family who invited me to spend my first Christmas in America with them, and have included me in their lives ever since. I will never forget all of his support to me, either when I needed someone to talk to, help me solve a dilemma or even help me pack up my bags or unpack them. He is someone that bridges the gap for me in multiple ways and I have learned a lot from him. I cannot ask for a better friend.

I would like to thank Don and Jean, who I refer to as my American parents. They took me in one cold, winter night and haven't let me go since! We are together for every holiday and birthday and they continue to support and champion me along the way. Thank you!

I would like to thank Dr. Joseph, who was my first Karate instructor in America and who cared enough about me to be willing to be my sponsor on my student visa application, as well as help me in my first days of training with them, even giving me 100 USD for meals when he knew I didn't have enough!

I would like to thank my three Mike's: the nurse, the trainer, and the roofer, who were amazing blessings to my life! They all played an incredible role in helping me along the way and I am so grateful for that.

I would like to thank some wonderful couples that have shared their love and wisdom with my wife and I: Ray and Elena, John and Mary, Tony and Brenda, Willy and Zully, Michael and Nimol, Jay and Andrea and Jeff and Cheryl.

I am so grateful for the moments of laughter or tears, over breakfasts, lunches and dinners with a lot of friends. I'm so thankful for them, whether I get to see them often, rarely, or perhaps never again, as we all come across each other's paths for a reason, a season or forever. I'd like to thank: Joe, Thomas, Richard, Phil, Daniel, Philip, Fataii, Roman, JeanMarques, Jordan, Greg, Newton, Jeff, Michael, John H., John B., John T., Tom, Nathan, Dale, Roberto, Tim, Rob, David M., Salah H., and many more friends, interpreters, neighbors and even strangers on the streets that we ended up having a nice, one-time conversation together about life! I came to Kansas City without knowing any of you and now I have the privilege of calling you friends. We can create a family anywhere we go in this world!

ABOUT THE AUTHOR

Nabil Cherif was born in Tunisia, migrated to several countries before settling in Kansas City in 2000. Nabil worked a variety of jobs, one of which was as an interpreter.

Fluent in French, Arabic, and English, Nabil witnessed first-hand the positive impacts of interpreting, one to be of service, but just as importantly, to be the bridge that helped others to not just be heard but understood.

In 2007, Bridging the Gap Interpreting, LLC was formed. Owning and operating a business was only the start, and over the years, Nabil has continued to grow both personally and professionally. He is a blackbelt martial artist and has trained extensively to become a certified personal trainer and transformation specialist with the International Sport Science Association.

Nabil is a certified motivational teacher and speaker with the John Maxwell Team. This book is his debut love letter to the world, focusing on entrepreneurship, experience and education, the integral foundations which support Nabil's passion to help others bridge gaps they encounter on their own personal journey.

And he's still passionate about hot dogs!

Bridging the Gap
INTERPRETING

PROFESSIONAL LANGUAGE SOLUTIONS

"Don't settle for being heard, when you can be understood"

-Nabil Cherif

OUR FOCUS

- Interpretation
- Translation
- Cultural Awareness Training
- Leadership Coaching

HAVE
QUESTIONS?

(913) 952-3739

office@kansascityinterpreting.com

Find us on social media!

LIVE INTERPRETATION
Whether you're needing **in-person** or virtual interpretation, we've got you covered in over 100 different languages!

DOCUMENT TRANSLATION
If you have a source document in one language, and need it converted to another, we can help! Your document will be converted with accuracy in both content and format.

CULTURAL AWARENESS TRAINING
Through curated training, we help companies navigate cultural barriers and prevent/resolve conflicts that could be caused by cultural misunderstandings.

LEADERSHIP COACHING
Leadership is a conscious process, and our individualized F.E.E.D. system aligns leaders' innate strengths and business objectives so they can lead and serve more effectively.

www.kansascityinterpreting.com

Made in the USA
Las Vegas, NV
13 February 2023

67410156R00154